Joyful Learning

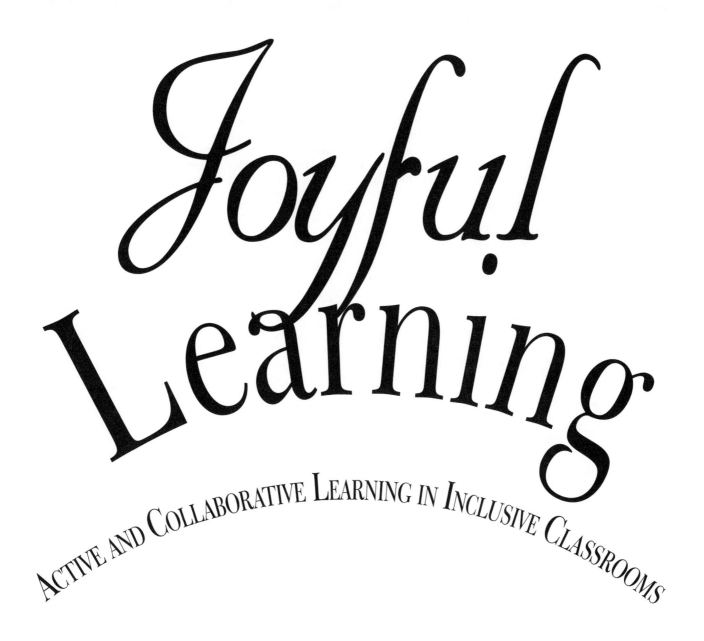

Joyful Learning

ACTIVE AND COLLABORATIVE LEARNING IN INCLUSIVE CLASSROOMS

Alice Udvari-Solner   Paula Kluth

CORWIN PRESS
A SAGE Company
Thousand Oaks, CA 91320

For information:

Corwin Press
A SAGE Company
2455 Teller Road
Thousand Oaks, California 91320
www.corwinpress.com

SAGE Ltd.
1 Oliver's Yard
55 City Road
London EC1Y 1SP
United Kingdom

SAGE India Pvt. Ltd.
B 1/I 1 Mohan Cooperative
    Industrial Area
Mathura Road, New Delhi 110 044
India

SAGE Asia-Pacific Pte. Ltd.
33 Pekin Street #02–01
Far East Square
Singapore 048763

Printed in the United States of America

Library of Congress Cataloging-in-Publication Data

Udvari-Solner, Alice.
Joyful learning:active and collaborative learning in inclusive classrooms/Alice Udvari-Solner, Paula Kluth.
    p. cm.
Includes bibliographical references and index.
ISBN 978-1-4129-4173-0 (cloth)
ISBN 978-1-4129-4174-7 (pbk.)
    1. Inclusive education—United States. 2. Activity programs in education—United States.
I. Kluth, Paula. II. Title.

LC1201.U38 2008
371.9′046—dc22   2007024840

This book is printed on acid-free paper.

08   09   10   11   10   9   8   7   6   5   4   3   2

Acquisitions Editor:	Allyson P. Sharp
Managing Editor:	David Chao
Editorial Assistant:	Mary Dang
Production Editor:	Libby Larson
Copy Editor:	Julie Gwin
Typesetter:	C & M Digitals (P) Ltd.
Proofreader:	Theresa Kay
Indexer:	Michael Ferreira
Cover Designer:	Lisa Miller

Contents

Preface

In our work in inclusive schools, we often talk to teachers about a variety of ways they can develop curriculum and instruction to be more responsive to the diverse learners in their classrooms. For many reasons, one of the practices we feel is the most "tried and true" for achieving this goal is the use of active and collaborative learning.

One reason we promote this type of instruction is related to student response. We find that students (including those in our own university classrooms) react very positively to active and collaborative learning techniques and that this type of teaching lends itself well to differentiation and individualization of instruction. Furthermore, in our observation, students are more engaged and seemingly comprehend more when they have agency in the learning process.

We are also drawn to instruction that is interactive and multilevel, because research indicates that students learn better when they are able to make meaning and demonstrate what they know. In fact, a multiyear study that Alice (the first author of this text) conducted about educators' responses to diverse learners indicated that when teachers created more responsive classrooms by changing lesson formats, teaching strategies, and instructional arrangements, the engagement, participation, and interactions of students with severe disabilities increased significantly (Udvari-Solner, 1995). Interestingly, research and related literature indicate other populations such as students with identified gifts and talents, those from diverse cultural backgrounds, and learners at the college level benefit similarly, showing increased interest, retention, and participation (Bonwell & Eisen, 1991; Cole, 2001; Harry & Klingner, 2005; Johnson, D. W., Johnson, & Smith, 1998; Marzano, 2003; Tomlinson, 2003).

Finally, we feel that these strategies are helpful in facilitating and supporting the collaboration of professionals. When we use active and collaborative learning structures in elementary and secondary classrooms, it is easy to plan ways for related service providers (e.g., speech therapists, occupational therapists), fellow classroom teachers (e.g., English as a Second Language professionals, general and special educators), and paraprofessionals to coteach and support all students. When students engage in a very busy and social structure such as *Dinner Party* (p. 42), for instance, we often ask speech therapists to work with small groups on pragmatics and vocabulary development. When we use text-based techniques such as *Say Something* (p. 68), we often collaborate with reading specialists, asking them to work with different groups of students throughout the lesson, so that all learners can gain more powerful comprehension strategies.

For all of these reasons, we began collecting active and collaborative learning structures and working with practicing educators and preservice teachers to adapt these different structures to meet the needs of a wider variety of students. As we shared these techniques in our classes and inservice presentations, teachers and university students alike asked us where they could find more information on using the adapted structures in their inclusive classes. These requests led us to develop this resource, which includes active learning techniques appropriate for use in K–12 classrooms and ideas for adapting or extending the activities for a wide range of learners in today's inclusive classrooms.

Although many of the structures featured are not new in the sense that we created or named them (in fact, some are purposely included because they are already popular with teachers and used in elementary and secondary classrooms), we feel this book is unique in that many texts related to active learning or differentiated instruction do not include information or ideas useful for today's diverse and inclusive classrooms; fail to consider the needs of learners with disabilities, especially those with significant disabilities; and lack specific suggestions for differentiating activities for the range of learners in a typical class. Alternatively, *Joyful Learning* focuses explicitly on inclusive classrooms; provides unique suggestions for meeting the needs of students with disabilities, including those with learning, cognitive, and sensory differences; contains dozens of familiar and novel activities that all students can access; and illustrates ways all students can participate in them.

USING THIS BOOK

The activities in this book are clearly intended for or at least well suited for use in classrooms in which students may have marked differences in ability, need, language, culture, or learning profile. We are hoping that by creating this resource, we are also promoting the idea that students with such differences can and should learn side by side.

How the Text Is Organized

The introduction to the book explores how inclusive schooling, differentiated instruction, and active learning are (or should be) linked and related. The five chapters that follow describe 50 structures that can be used with students in both elementary and secondary schools.

Please note that we have attempted to organize the structures into logical categories to help the reader locate techniques that match an instructional purpose. However, we don't believe the categories are mutually exclusive, and many structures can be employed for multiple instructional uses. Therefore, consider the chapter headings simply as a guide; readers should feel free to be flexible in how they apply all of the strategies. The five chapters are as follows:

1. **"Building Teams and Classroom Communities."** This initial chapter includes techniques that help teachers build community and teaming. These structures promote relationship building, listening, sharing, and interdependence.

2. **"Teaching and Learning."** This chapter contains structures that help students of all ages learn standards-based content in meaningful, interesting, and compelling ways. This collection of ideas will help learners remember information, teach content to one another, and make discoveries about course content.

3. **"Studying and Reviewing."** The study and review structures give teachers ideas for supporting students as they work independently or with small groups to prepare for assessments or to learn familiar content in a deeper way.

4. **"Creating Active Lectures."** Every teacher needs to engage in whole-class instruction and lecture-based instruction at some point during the school day. This instruction does not need to be formal and dry, however. By using the structures outlined in this chapter, teachers can involve their students in whole-class learning without losing students who need a more personalized approach.

5. **"Assessing and Celebrating."** Structures offered in this chapter will give educators active-learning options for assessing student understanding, sharing learning, and celebrating growth.

Each one of these chapters features 10 activities. Each structure is outlined in detail with directions, reproducible handouts (when applicable), classroom-tested examples, and guidelines for maximizing the participation of students. Some structures also feature tips for implementation and ideas for extending or varying the structure.

Using the Structures

This book is best used as a co-planning tool between general educators and specialists (i.e., special educators, occupational therapists, speech clinicians, physical therapists, etc.). We recommend that all team members who share responsibility for the same students become familiar with the structures and the associated procedures. In our research, we found that when members of educational teams used the same language and understood the same techniques, joint planning for differentiation was expedited (Udvari-Solner, 1996a). Effective supports for students with learning differences occur when instructional teams meet on a consistent basis (i.e., weekly or biweekly) and determine what is important for students to learn and how best to organize that learning. Familiarity with the structures in this book by all team members will provide an abundance of options for reaching those students who challenge us the most as educators.

If you don't currently have strong collaborative partnerships, using these structures can be an effective way to begin such a relationship. In our preservice courses, we often suggest that special educators or therapists seeking to coteach or to further develop their inclusive schooling model should offer to demonstrate active and collaborative structures as a way into the general education classroom. A general education classroom teacher who seems less than enthusiastic about making changes in curriculum or instruction often can be inspired to do so when alternatives to traditional teaching are not only suggested but also modeled. Such an offer illustrates that all adults in the building can and should teach and that it is not just the job of the general educator to take on new roles.

Keep in mind that teachers aren't the only ones who should use these structures. We feel strongly that as educators, we are modeling techniques that we want our students to use and incorporate into their own instructional repertoire. There may be times when it is appropriate for a student or group of students to lead a class discussion or present reports or individual research. These techniques can be used to enliven this process and give students yet another arena for building skills and developing competencies.

In addition, if you are a principal, department chairperson, or even superintendent, consider using these structures in your meetings and staff development activities. There is no better way to emphasize a commitment to and enthusiasm for active and collaborative learning than to model it in your own work. Furthermore, because teachers are learners too, you are likely to get a higher quality of participation in meetings when you are using techniques that will reach and interest larger numbers of "students."

For instance, a middle-school principal had his staff try out the *Group Resumé* activity (p. 4) during a summer staff development institute. Teachers were mixed into groups with those from different grade levels and specialty areas and asked to construct the resumé on large pieces of chart paper. This activity gave the teachers the opportunity to learn about the skills and competencies of one another and, ultimately, helped them get and give support to one another on topics ranging from cooperative learning, to conducting classroom meetings, to developing an in-classroom volunteer program. The resumés were then posted around the room and used as a springboard for the next activity, which was to develop an action plan for learning from colleagues.

Finally, consider this book as a vehicle for professional development. Teaching has been called one of the loneliest professions, and unfortunately, in some schools, trying something new in the classroom can make a teacher feel apprehensive and even isolated. We believe there is strength in numbers and that being creative in the classroom should be supported and celebrated in the school community. In healthy organizations, new information and innovative practices are shared in collaborative ways. One way to facilitate this shift in school culture is to initiate professional development that focuses on the use of active and collaborative structures to differentiate instruction. This type of staff development can be as simple as a book study group or as organized as a formal action research project. Some schools with which we have worked arranged for a group of interested faculty to meet weekly or biweekly while reading a draft of this book. In this setting, teachers selected structures of interest and agreed to implement one or two within the week. In each subsequent meeting, teachers shared their successes and challenges. This informal arrangement also provided a time for educators to bring forward concerns about key students and to collectively generate methods of differentiation in the use of the structures.

Getting started: Tips for implementing the structures. Begin using these structures in your unit or lesson planning with particular students in mind. Effective differentiation occurs when we consider our learners and find out about their abilities, preferences, and areas of intelligence as a starting point in instructional design. Specific structures should be selected to match the needs of students in your classroom, promote the skills you want to foster, and in some cases, provide opportunities to achieve social and academic goals that are a part of a learner's individualized education plan (IEP). For example, a student with learning disabilities needs multiple trials to retain information and also has an IEP goal to paraphrase key concepts from texts. From the selection of active learning structures, *Popcorn* (p. 58) might be chosen as a review strategy for the entire class. This structure requires students to summarize key learning in their own words and then teach or share the same content several times to changing partners. By using this structure, the lesson now provides avenues for the student with learning disabilities to work on critical goals identified by his or her educational team.

Keep in mind that all of the structures can be used individually, or they can be "stacked" to create new and different classroom experiences. For instance, a teacher might use the aforementioned *Popcorn* structure to get students talking about content and follow that activity with *The Whip* (p. 91) to find out one thing that each student learned from his or her classmates during the interview process. Or she might use *Take My Perspective, Please!* (p. 96) to get students to share their opinions or impressions about a topic and follow that with *Stand and Deliver* (p. 85) to allow students to share one thing they learned from their interactions.

Making them work for all: Tips for adapting and teaching the structures. These structures are not subject or grade-level specific. We offer examples with each structure; however, if the example does not mirror your exact teaching experience, we encourage you to be inventive. The structures can be used in different ways across subject areas and with students of different ages, so they should definitely be edited, changed, and modified to fit not only your grade level but also fit your unique classroom of students.

Our suggestions throughout this book for modifying, adapting, and otherwise altering the activities are not comprehensive; we intend these ideas simply to serve as examples as to how certain activities might be changed for various types of learners and, perhaps more important, that they should be changed! In other words, we hope to communicate that adaptation, differentiation, and personalization of lessons for all students is what good teachers do. Furthermore, we are striving to demonstrate that when we expand or alter an activity to meet the needs of a single learner or a small group of learners, the result is almost always a lesson that is more comprehensive, responsive, and appropriate—for all. In Table 0.1, we have provided a short list of simple and quick ways to differentiate instruction when using active and collaborative learning structures. More extensive ideas are offered in the section of each structure titled "Methods to Maximize Engagement and Participation."

To further increase your chances of meeting the needs of all learners, we recommend practice, practice, practice. Remember that no matter how you use these structures and no matter what age group you teach, you will undoubtedly need to model the structures (more than once), review how to use them, and integrate them regularly into your week, month, and year. We often hear concerns from teachers that students will not like engaging in a different

Table 0.1   Quick and Easy Ways to Differentiate When Using Collaborative and Active Learning Structures

- Have students work in pairs.

- Bring therapists, paraprofessionals, other teachers, or volunteers into the classroom to help facilitate the activity and to give all students more adult support.

- Give directions or review the content in advance (preteach).

- Allow all or some students to practice the activity in advance, or videotape the structure so the learner can see and hear what is expected.

- Allow students to have cue cards or previewed materials during activities.

- Allow students to have different roles in the activities; if most students are talking in small groups, one or two students might document responses they hear or serve as facilitators of all the groups.

- Ask or allow all students to use alternative or augmentative types of communication; you might, for instance, give all students the option to either speak or write a response during a group sharing activity.

- Give choices in the activity (e.g., let students switch partners or stay with the same partner).

- Provide "wait time" or "think time" to one or all students before expecting a response.

- Use pictures as well as words when giving directions or when engaging in activities with written information.

- Ask students to help in preparing the lessons so they can take active roles in leading activities, generating questions or content, and even creating adaptations for one another.

method of learning, that it will detract from the content, or that it will take too long to carry out the activity. For all of these reasons, it is very important to not only show students the structures but also teach how to use them (this may be particularly important for students with learning difficulties or those who struggle with change or novelty). Avoid the common error of using these structures as beginning-of-the-year icebreakers, and only as beginning-of-the-year icebreakers. These structures, in most cases, are designed to be used as tools for delivering daily instruction, and with regular use, student responses will become more proficient and self-directed. Be sure to explain to students why you are doing what you are doing, how it is relevant to the content, and how the activity will proceed. Students may resist learning this way, particularly if they have not had opportunities to do so in the past; this is a natural part of the learning process.

Be patient, enjoy the process, and give yourself—and your students—time to learn the structures and the new way of doing business in the classroom.

CONCLUSIONS

In sum, we hope we have created a text that you, the reader, will find useful. More than that, however, we hope that we have created a tool that might help many of you create classrooms that are inviting and accessible for a larger variety of learners. Although we do want this text to serve as a quick, desktop lesson planning reference, we are also hoping that it can inspire changes in classroom practice and in the number of students who receive access to meaningful curriculum and instruction in general education classrooms.

If you find this text useful, and particularly if it helps you support students with unique learning profiles, reach students who have not traditionally had success in the classroom, or create more inclusive opportunities for students with disabilities, please write and let us know (Alice Udvari-Solner, alice@education.wisc.edu, and Paula Kluth, pkluth@earthlink.net). We are interested in learning more about the potential of active instruction as a response to if not a remedy for everything from challenging behavior, to boredom, to academic struggles. Good luck—we wish you success and we hope to hear from you!

ACKNOWLEDGMENTS

Many people helped us in the conceptualization and completion of this manuscript, but before we thank those who made the writing of the book possible, we must share our gratitude for the students with disabilities and many other learners with unique learning styles who have helped us think critically about differentiating instruction and adapting curriculum. Although we have both taught dozens of learners who have guided our thinking in this respect, we are especially indebted to Mattie, Mark, Sarah, Sherrie, Paul, Jason, Franklin, Joe, Andrew, and Bob.

We would also like to thank the schools that have welcomed us into their classrooms to teach and be taught. Many educators field tested these strategies with us and fearlessly entered into an exploration of their own practice with students and colleagues alike. We are especially grateful to the staff members and administrators from Chicago Public Schools; Greenwich Public Schools in Greenwich, Connecticut; Madison Metropolitan School District in Madison, Wisconsin; Highland Park High School in Highland Park, Illinois; Deerfield High School in Deerfield, Illinois; and Verona High School in Verona, Wisconsin. In particular, we want to acknowledge the creativity and innovation of Matthew Armfield and Dr. Jeff Hoyer, teachers who contributed several ideas to this text and inspire us with their creativity in the classroom and commitment to students.

The work of many colleagues has shaped our thinking about curricular adaptations, differentiating instruction, active learning, and inclusive schooling, but we would like to acknowledge a few of them in particular. Dr. Lou Brown acted as our teacher and guide as we trained to be educators. He acknowledged and fostered our ability and desire to teach all children and to hold a steadfast vision of an inclusive society. He cultivated an urgent sense of advocacy in us to question the status quo, to reinvent conceptions of schooling, and to keep children with disabilities and their families at the center of decision making.

Dr. Jacqueline Thousand and Dr. Richard Villa have been generous mentors and comrades in our professional and personal lives. Their prolific work in the development of inclusive education provided not only the big ideas but also the practical steps to make change in complex systems. We thank them for inviting us along in the journey, sharing professional opportunities, and promoting our writing in the field early in our careers.

We extend extra-special gratitude to our friend and colleague, Patrick "Paco" Schwarz, who constantly inspires us to think differently, to innovate, to ask better questions, and to bring energy and fun to the classroom, and into our lives. You help us dream of possibilities!

The inspiration for the content of this book emanated from the ideas and the writings of Mel Silberman, Merrill Harmin, Spencer Kagan, and Mara Sapon-Shevin. We are grateful for the work they have done that has made such a positive impact in the fields of teaching and learning and curriculum and instruction.

These acknowledgments would not be complete without mentioning the hard work and innovation of our students from the University of Wisconsin–Madison, Syracuse University, and National-Louis University. So much of this material comes from our experiences teaching future educators; we are grateful to our students for asking critical questions and for working as change agents in public schools every day.

Our spouses and children supported our work on this project by allowing us to write, proofread, edit, and chat on the phone on evenings and weekends. Madda and Haven were especially helpful in answering our questions about elementary school curriculum and sharing ideas on what is cool, what is interesting, and what helps kids learn.

Finally, we are grateful to those at Corwin Press for the time and care they invested in this project. In particular, we extend our very best to Allyson Sharp, Kathleen McLane, and Mary Dang, who were patient and helpful every step of the way.

Corwin Press gratefully acknowledges the contributions of the following reviewers:

Sharon Gonder
Retired Learning Disabilities
    Teacher K–12
Educational Consultant
Editor, Osage Bend Publishing Co.
Jefferson City, MO

Kelli Kercher
Transition/Inclusion Specialist
Special Education Department
Murray School District
Murray, UT

Karen Landress
Exceptional Needs Teacher
MILA Elementary
Brevard County Schools
Merritt Island, FL

Melinda Pierson
Professor of Special Education
California State University
Fullerton, CA

About the Authors

 **Alice Udvari-Solner** is a national consultant in education and holds an appointment at the University of Wisconsin–Madison in the Department of Curriculum and Instruction. The graduate and undergraduate courses she teaches on the topic of accommodating diverse learners in general education settings are integral to the elementary, secondary, and special education teacher certification programs. Differentiation, the design of effective curricular adaptations, collaborative team work among educators and paraprofessionals, and systems change toward inclusive education are areas that are central to her research and teaching. Dr. Udvari-Solner's recent research has focused on the development of the Universal Design Process for Differentiation—a method used to promote co-planning among educators to design responsive strategies for diverse learners.

 **Paula Kluth** is an independent scholar and education consultant. Her professional and research interests center on supporting students with autism and significant disabilities in inclusive classrooms and differentiating instruction. Dr. Kluth is the author of *"You're Going to Love This Kid": Teaching Students With Autism in the Inclusive Classroom*; the lead editor of *Access to Academics for All: Critical Approaches to Inclusive Curriculum, Instruction, and Policy* (with Diana Straut and Douglas Biklen); and the co-author of *"A Land We Can Share": Teaching Literacy to Students With Autism* (with Kelly Chandler-Olcott); and *You're Welcome: 30 Innovative Ideas for the Inclusive Classroom* (with Patrick Schwarz). To learn more about Paula, visit her personal Web site: www.paulakluth.com.

To our children—Madda, Haven, Erma, and Willa—who bring so much joy

Introduction

Facilitating Inclusive Education Through Active and Collaborative Learning

R ecently, we spoke with the mother of a young man with Down syndrome, who was frustrated about her son's experience in middle school. Bryan, the young man, had been learning and fully participating in all aspects of classroom life at his inclusive middle school when the family moved across town to a different school that was also deemed inclusive. Before the move, the family was incredibly impressed with the education Bryan was receiving. His mother explained that Bryan was asking and answering questions during whole-class instruction, working effectively in cooperative groups, completing assigned projects, taking a leadership role in class meetings, entering the science fair annually, participating in school concerts and performances, and establishing positive social relationships with classmates without disabilities.

After the move, however, the young man's interest in school faded. The new school, although in the same district as the old and serving essentially the same population of learners, had a more traditional educational philosophy. Students were expected to sit in their desks for longer periods of time during large-group instruction and engage in more independent work. The principal explained that although the school was committed to inclusive education, they recommended it only for learners who "could handle it." In this school, he explained that learning "was taken seriously" and the teachers taught in more traditional ways to "cover all the material." Bryan began struggling, and before long, teachers were recommending that he be pulled out of their classes. Bryan's attitude toward school changed and, for the first time ever, he started resisting doing his homework, getting up in the morning, and even going to school.

Unfortunately, the scenario described by this mother is all too common; under one set of circumstances, her son is learning, is meeting individual goals, and is effectively included. Yet, in another setting, her son is seemingly unable to negotiate the general education curriculum and instruction. As researchers and teacher educators in the field of inclusive schooling, we have been interested in and concerned about why these discrepancies in outcomes for students occur between different classrooms. Over the course of our work with educators across the country, we have attempted to examine what conditions, practices, and approaches facilitate the effective inclusion of students with diverse learning needs (Kasa-Hendrickson & Kluth, 2005; Kluth, 2003, 2004; Kluth, Straut, & Biklen, 2003; Udvari-Solner, 1993, 1995, 1996a, 1996b, 2003; Udvari-Solner & Thousand, 1996; Udvari-Solner, Villa, & Thousand, 2002, 2005).

We have consistently observed that students struggle not because they cannot learn the content but because they cannot learn in the way they are being taught. Too often, we expect students to change or to leave our classrooms when they experience failure or are disengaged. More often, we should be examining the classroom itself, questioning our teaching approaches and curriculum, and evaluating all the ways we might support, engage, respond to, and challenge every student. In other words, we should be following the key principles that underlie inclusive education (Falvey, Givner, & Kimm, 1995; Fisher & Roach, 1999; Fisher, Sax, & Pumpian, 1999; Jorgensen, 1998; Kluth, 2003; Sapon-Shevin, 2007; Udvari-Solner & Thousand, 1996; Villa & Thousand, 2005).

WHAT IS INCLUSIVE SCHOOLING?

Udvari-Solner and Thousand (1996) defined inclusive education as "a value-based practice that attempts to bring all students, including those with disabilities, into full membership with their local school" (p. 182). Inclusive education complements other school reform efforts by calling for a critique of existing school, teaching, and classroom culture. Administrators, parents, and educators are encouraged to question and reinvent traditional teaching paradigms and replace them with practices that value and encourage every student as a participatory member of the classroom community (Udvari-Solner, 1997). This progressive educational movement has evolved over the course of nearly 30 years, and key principles or tenets are well established to guide its practice. Specifically, in inclusive schools, we should see separate or segregated settings for instruction of students with differences begin to be dismantled. We should also notice that support services are being brought to the general education classroom and support personnel are becoming integral members of teaching teams in general education environments. Most important to daily classroom practice, in inclusive schools, we should observe that curriculum and instruction are collaboratively designed by special and general educators (and, when appropriate, therapists, English as a Second Language teachers, facilitators of enrichment programs, reading specialists, and others) with the intent to differentiate methods and materials for learning.

WHAT IS DIFFERENTIATED INSTRUCTION?

Scholars and practitioners have used many different terms to describe *differentiation*, or the design of curriculum, instruction, and assessment that meet the needs of diverse learners. In 1995, Udvari-Solner proposed a reflective decision-making model for rethinking classroom practices and creating what was then referred to as "curricular adaptations" to better accommodate all students. Oyler (2001) used the term *accessible instruction* to describe the use of democratic practices and the development of challenging learning experiences.

Udvari-Solner, Villa, and Thousand (2002, 2005) extended this thinking by proposing a framework for differentiation called the Universal Design Process, which requires advance decisions about the content, process, and products of learning so that flexible and multiple approaches for teaching and learning are incorporated at the onset of lesson design.

In this same time frame, Tomlinson (1995) was promoting similar ideas and methods in her seminal book, *Differentiating Instruction in a Mixed-Ability Classroom*. It was this text that popularized the phrase *differentiated instruction*, and soon thereafter, researchers, educators, and school leaders began using this term as a catch-all for methods that are designed to reach, teach, and challenge a wide range of learners. Specifically, Tomlinson (1995) defined differentiation in this way:

> At its most basic level, differentiating instruction means "shaking up" what goes on in the classroom so that students have multiple options for taking in information, making sense of ideas, and expressing what they learn. In other words, a differentiated classroom provides different avenues to acquiring content, processing or making sense of ideas, and to developing products. (p. 3)

We like Tomlinson's definition and feel it has moved educators beyond thinking about curricular change as something that happens only in relation to disability. This definition also demystified the idea of differentiation, making change less threatening and more "do-able" in classrooms.

Recently, however, we have been inspired by teachers in the field to expand on Tomlinson's (1995) definition of differentiation. Over the past several years, we have been asking educators to articulate the influences and philosophies that have guided their work in their inclusive classrooms (Kasa-Hendrickson & Kluth, 2005; Udvari-Solner, 1996b). When asked about their practices, these teachers provide a fairly complex and political picture of what it means to meet the needs of all learners. From those conversations, we have constructed this definition:

> Differentiation requires a desire to honor the individual. It is a conscious and critical act that calls into question what we teach, why we should teach it, and how we expect students to learn. Teachers attend not only to curriculum, instruction, and assessment, but also to issues of relevance, meaning, and respect. A student's individual needs, experiences, and interests influence the design of learning experiences. The presence of difference in the classroom is not viewed as a liability but as the necessary catalyst for changes that will improve instruction for all.

Inherent in this definition and in Tomlinson's (1995) version is the need to look closely at and reconsider the process of teaching and learning, in other words, the way we teach. Specifically, we should attend to how we understand and respond to our learners and how students experience their education. Do they feel they are giving or only getting information? Do they have opportunities to demonstrate what they know and can do? Do they care about what they are learning? Are daily experiences fun or at least satisfying? These questions have caused us to turn our attention specifically to differentiating via collaborative and active learning.

Some form of active or collaborative learning is identified as a core tenet of most differentiation or curricular adaptations models. There are certainly many other methods used to differentiate that should be employed regularly, including using coteaching, using flexible grouping, adapting materials, making adjustments in expectations and goals, tiering lessons, and overlapping curriculum. However, we find that when teachers consciously engineer active and collaborative learning approaches, many more avenues to access the general education curriculum are created for the diverse student populations that we serve in our classrooms every day.

WHAT ARE ACTIVE LEARNING AND COLLABORATIVE LEARNING?

We believe that the use of both active and collaborative approaches achieves positive outcomes by promoting student dignity and empowerment, facilitating self-management, attending to a sense of community, and increasing the energy and awareness of both teachers and students. These are outcomes we feel are essential to successful inclusive classrooms and that we are, therefore, trying to promote. In this book, we use the term *active and collaborative learning* to describe all of the featured structures because they incorporate elements of both types of instruction (active learning and collaborative learning).

Active Learning

Active learning involves putting students at the center of instruction and giving them opportunities to solve, explore, experiment, try, create, and invent. In classrooms that promote active learning, students are often moving, sharing, working in and out of their seats, using a range of materials, and engaging with others while talking or thinking aloud. Active learning is, essentially then, anything that students do in a classroom other than merely passively listening to the teacher's instruction. This includes everything from listening practices that help the students absorb what they hear, to brief writing exercises in which students react to lecture material, to short games used for review and introduction of content, to complex group exercises in which students apply course material to authentic or real-life situations or past experiences.

Collaborative Learning

Collaborative learning is a philosophy and technique of interaction that is rooted in constructivist and social learning theories (Bandura, 1977; Panitz, 1997; Vygotsky, 1978). It is a process by which students interact in pairs or groups with intent to solicit and respect the abilities and contributions of individual members. Typically, authority and responsibility are shared for group actions and outcomes (Panitz, 1997).

Collaborative learning changes the dynamics of the classroom by requiring discussion among learners. Students are encouraged to question the curriculum and attempt to create personal meaning before an adult interprets what is important to learn. Opportunities to organize, clarify, elaborate, or practice information are engineered, and listening, disagreeing, and expressing ideas are as important as the "right answers." Furthermore, in classrooms that encourage this type of ideology, the student is an active participant in learning rather than a passive recipient of education from an expert source.

Why Use Active and Collaborative Learning?

Historically, active learning and collaborative methods have been promoted and celebrated by a host of well-respected educators including Socrates, Booker T. Washington, John Dewey, Paulo Freire, Maria Montessori, and more recently, Howard Gardner. Yet education in many American classrooms still tends to be primarily a passive venture. Students are often asked to sit in desks for long periods of time and learn through what Freire (1970) deemed "banking education." In this method, the teacher teaches and the students are taught, the teacher knows everything and the students know nothing, the teacher thinks and the students are thought about, the teacher talks and the students listen, the teacher chooses and the students comply, and the teacher is the subject of the learning process and the pupils are the objects (Freire, 1970).

Freire (1970) dismissed banking education as dehumanizing and called for a different kind of learning. He promoted instead a student-centered and relevant curriculum; a multicultural, democratic, and dynamic pedagogy; and a safe, tolerant, sensitive, and active learning environment. He felt that education should be pursued collaboratively, with student and teacher working in concert to teach and learn. Furthermore, he insisted that learners do not enter into the process of learning by memorizing facts, but by constructing their reality in engaging, dialoging, and problem solving with others (Freire, 1970; Gadotti, 1994).

Freire (1970) believed in the power of active and collaborative learning and for good reason. Research at all levels of schooling has indicated that students learn and retain more when they have agency in the process and have opportunities to speak, listen, share, interact, reflect, and move. In a well-known study, Ruhl, Hughes, and Schloss (1987) set out to explore what happens when students are given opportunities to make meaning of classroom content. In the study, two groups of university students received the same instruction in two different ways. In the experimental group, an instructor paused for two minutes on three occasions (intervals between pauses were approximately 15 minutes) during each of five lectures. During the pauses, while students worked in pairs to discuss and rework their notes, no interaction occurred between instructor and students. At the end of each lecture, students were given three minutes to write down everything they could remember from the lesson. Then, 12 days after the last lecture, students were also given a multiple-choice test to measure long-term retention. A control group received the same lectures as those in the "pause procedure" group and was similarly tested. In two separate courses repeated over two semesters, the results were consistent and telling. Students who experienced more interaction and were more involved in the learning process did significantly better on the daily assessments and on the final multiple-choice test. In fact, the magnitude of the difference in mean scores between the two groups was large enough to make a difference of two letter grades. This study suggests, therefore, that if teachers talk less (even *six minutes* less as in the aforementioned study) students can learn *more*! This finding is counterintuitive, as most teachers believe that student learning is boosted when more material is covered, not less.

In a related study, medical school professors prepared three different lectures on the same subject; one lecture was considered "high-density," another was considered "medium-density," and the third was considered "low-density" (Russell, Hendricson, & Herbert, 1984). Ninety percent of the sentences in the high-density lecture represented new information, 70% of the sentences in the medium-density lecture represented new information, and 50% of the low-density lecture represented new information. During the pieces of the lecture when new material was not being presented, the instructor reinforced material by repeating important ideas, highlighting the significance of the material, providing examples related to the content, and relating the material to the students' lives and experiences. Finally, students were given (a) a pretest (that showed no significant difference in their knowledge base), (b) a posttest immediately after the lecture, and (c) an unannounced posttest 15 days later.

Statistical results clearly showed that students in this study learned and retained lecture information better when the density of new material was low. The implication is that the amount of new information that students can learn in a given time is limited and that we defeat our purposes when we exceed that limit. In other words, teachers would be better off presenting only a few significant pieces of information and spending the rest of their time engaged in activities designed to reinforce the material in students' minds.

These two studies indicate that teachers are working against lesson objectives when they resist methods that are student centered and responsive. More than one teacher has told us that he or she doesn't have time for active learning because of the standards or the amount of content that must be covered. The truth, for these teachers, is that they can't afford not to use active learning in their teaching if they want students to learn and remember an ever-increasing number of facts, figures, ideas, and concepts.

Even the best and most entertaining lecturers begin to lose the attention of the audience within 15 to 20 minutes. A well-known study of information retention illustrates this point. Hartley and Davies (1978) demonstrated that immediately after a lecture, students recalled about 70% of the content presented during the first 10 minutes and 20% of the content of the last 10 minutes. More recent brain research (Jensen, 1998) reinforces these findings indicating that continuous, intense attention to external sources can be sustained for only 10 minutes or less. Also, to promote and focus attention, regular "mental breaks" lasting anywhere from 5 to 20 minutes multiple times a day are needed (Howard, 1994; Rossi & Nimmons, 1991).

We believe the active and collaborative learning strategies presented in this book provide the vehicles for teachers to build in processing breaks, time for learners to imprint material, and the use of the structures create the social culture necessary for constructing new knowledge and responses that are critical to advance student learning. Of course, more effective teaching and learning are not the only benefits of using active learning (although they are quite significant outcomes). Teachers profit in active and collaborative classrooms too. Educators often complain (for good reason) that they do not have opportunities to observe their students, work with individuals, or listen to the everyday "buzz" of the classroom. In other words, teachers feel that they cannot engage in many of the activities that would benefit their teaching because they are too busy leading the group. When teachers use active and collaborative learning techniques, however, they have more opportunities to try new roles and take on new responsibilities. Teachers who no longer need to be the constant "sage on the stage" are free during active learning exercises to interact with students, ask and answer questions, teach mini-lessons to individuals or small groups, and even stand back and watch students to evaluate their learning.

Beyond the pedagogical benefits, active and collaborative learning make lessons much more enjoyable for both students and teachers. Educators have revealed that when students who are accustomed to active learning begin working in their groups or engaging in a familiar game or structure, the entire mood and feel of the classroom changes. The volume rises, students are talking, interactions that might not happen spontaneously occur, laughter is common, and everyone has an opportunity to contribute and to learn.

Our explicit goal for this text is that it is used to create more classrooms like the one described in the previous paragraph; we hope that these structures can help teachers better respond to *all* of their students and create more inclusive, supportive, inspired, and, of course, joyful classroom environments.

Building Teams and Classroom Communities

1

 ## THAT'S THE STORY OF MY LIFE!

Although many celebrated figures have the unique (and probably transforming) opportunity to share their biography, ordinary people typically do not have the chance to tell their life stories. This activity allows students to share some of their personal history and to develop new connections with classmates.

Directions

- Initially, students will work individually. Ask each of them to take a piece of flipchart paper and fold it into quarters so it is shaped like a book.
- Then, on the front cover of their creation, have students write the title of their story. To add a bit of whimsy to this part of the activity, you might instruct them to choose the title of a popular novel, song, movie, or television program (e.g., *I Did It My Way*, *The Fast and Furious Life of George*, *Wendy's "Believe It or Not" Life Story*).
- On the inside of the front cover (page 2), have students list an index of their lives, including
  - Date and place of birth
  - Family information (number of siblings, names of pets)
  - Favorite hobby, sport, or interest
  - Favorite quote, phrase, or joke
  - Most exciting moment
  - Thing that makes them unique
- On page 3, ask students to draw a picture of their perfect day.
- Finally, on the back cover of the book, students should draw a picture of their future (family, where they are living, what they are doing).
- When all books are complete, have each student tell their story using the book as a visual aid. Depending on the size of the class, you may want to have students share stories in small groups.
- If possible, leave the books in a central location for the day or for the week so classmates can learn more about one another.

Examples

- A high school French teacher asked second-year students to construct stories using only the vocabulary they had learned the previous year. Then she asked them to read their stories to one another, again using only the French they had mastered to date. Thus, the exercise served not only as a community building exercise but as a review of vocabulary and as an opportunity to polish their conversational skills.

- One elementary school teacher used this structure as a getting-to-know-you exercise during a year when she was welcoming Beth, a student with multiple disabilities, into her classroom. When Beth's mother asked if she should come and explain her child's abilities, strengths, history, and special needs to the rest of the children, the teacher decided it would be nice for all students to learn this type of information about one another. She wanted to make sure that Beth and the other students understood that all learners in the classroom were unique and special. Students spent a day collecting information for their books; this collection process involved interviewing family and friends, gathering artifacts from home, and filling in a teacher-prepared questionnaire designed as a brainstorming tool. Then, they worked alone (or in pairs, if assistance was needed) to construct their books. The school social worker visited the class to help students tell their stories and express themselves in words.

  The speech and language therapist also visited during this time to teach Beth some new sign language vocabulary related to the book; she also helped Beth answer all the necessary questions by using both the new signs and some pictures other students tore from magazines. Students spent two language arts periods sharing their work and asking and answering questions about their personal stories. Their books were then displayed in the school library.

- A high school psychology teacher used *That's the Story of My Life!* to give students opportunities to share personal information and to reinforce key concepts from his class. Students were asked to include the following pieces of information in their books:
  - Full name
  - Place of birth
  - Family information
  - Favorite hobby, sport, or interest
  - Favorite Web site
  - Theorist studied in class that most intrigued them (e.g., Freud, Piaget, Bandura)

  Students also had to include the results of a personality test the teacher had administered. They could choose to illustrate the results in some way or summarize them in narrative form. Finally, they took turns sharing their stories with assigned partners.

Methods to Maximize Engagement and Participation

- Tell or share the story of your own life; show students a sample storybook featuring your own family, interests, and dreams. If you are working with younger children and you are using this structure to teach about diversity, individuality, or community, you may even want to invite other adults into the classroom to read their stories so that learners can see and hear about differences related to gender, sexual identity, family structure, and cultural and ethnic background.

- Give students a brainstorming worksheet before having them complete the activity; some learners will need time and some structure to generate answers to the prompts.

- This activity might be the perfect opportunity for students who are new immigrants or those who are simply new to the school to reveal more about themselves, their families, and their culture. Consider allowing these learners to also bring in an artifact or two from their home to share as a way of extending their story and further illustrating their life experience. Bringing artifacts might also be helpful for students with more significant disabilities who struggle with written communication.

- Some students may need different materials to create their books; if there are learners in the classroom with fine motor problems who may struggle with drawing and writing, magazine pictures, rubber stamps, and clip-art images can be provided for students to use in the construction of their stories.

- You will want to consider how well students know each other when designing prompts; students who have worked together for years will be familiar with basic information about one another (e.g., full name, family structure) and may be more interested in gathering information about their classmates that is slightly more in-depth, such as their most embarrassing moment, their family traditions, or their travel experiences.

Ideas for Using This Structure in My Classroom ✒

_____

_____

_____

_____

_____

_____

_____

_____

_____

_____

GROUP RESUMÉ

Although resumés describe an individual's accomplishments, *Group Resumé* (Silberman, 1996) highlights the accomplishments of a team. Asking students to create a collective profile is an entertaining and effective way to promote reflection and self-assessment. The group resumé is a quick and easy team-building strategy; students not only find out about each other, but perhaps also about themselves.

This activity also guides students to focus on the classroom as a teaching and learning community and helps all learners understand the resources they have in their classmates. The resumés can be general or can be tailored to content (e.g., *The Catcher in the Rye* Club, the Timpani Three), and they can be used to start the year or to summarize learning at the end of a unit.

Directions

- Explain to students that the classroom includes students with many different talents, experiences, gifts, and interests.
- Divide students into small groups, and give every team chart paper or newsprint and colored markers.
- Ask each group to prepare a collective resumé to advertise their accomplishments.
- After giving the groups time to work on the project, invite them to present their resumés to the class.
- The resumés can then be left hanging for the rest of the day (or week or year) so that others can see the knowledge and abilities represented in the class.

Example

In a high school art class, the teacher asked students to summarize their end-of-the-year learning by creating group resumés (see Figure 1.1). Groups were instructed to focus, in particular, on what skills they had acquired during the year, what abilities they had gained, and what information they remembered from class discussions. One group of young women who developed an interest in Impressionist art during the year titled their resumé, "Women Who Leave an Impression."

Methods to Maximize Participation and Engagement

- To be sure that all students participate, the teacher should give learners ideas on how to elicit information from peers. Students could be shown how to informally interview one another and how to ask questions that will allow each of their group members to contribute something. For example, if a student claims she cannot think of anything to add, or if she does not have reliable expressive communication, the other team members might share their contributions first or give the student time to circulate around the room and get ideas from other teams, or let the student draw or sketch ideas instead of name them.
- In their small groups, have students generate a list of questions and conduct a round-robin interview of each other before assembling the resumé.

Figure 1.1   Group Resumé Example

Women Who Leave an Impression

Krisi, Nancy, Jen, Kana, Kim, and Katia

Qualifications

- Familiar with Impressionism
- Can compare/contrast Impressionism, Realism, and Cubism
- Can compare the styles of Impressionist painters (especially Renoir, Monet, Manet, and Degas)
- Have read autobiographies of Cassatt and Cezanne
- Have toured two major art museums including the Art Institute of Chicago
- Have successfully completed six high school art classes
- Knowledge of
  o Watercolor painting
  o Sculpture (wood and clay)
  o Furniture painting
  o Collage
  o Origami
  o Print making

Other Skills

- Sign language
- Wood carving
- Stomping
- Writing poetry
- Word processing
- Making beaded jewelry
- Sewing and designing clothes
- Making movies on the computer
- Can sing every song from *My Fair Lady*

Hobbies and Interests

- Reading, watching old movies, listening to music (especially movie soundtracks), going to Great America and other amusement parks, and karate

- If creating a traditional resumé is challenging for some, allow groups to opt for creating a video or audio resumé. Even with these alternate forms, however, remind students that their "document" should be both organized and brief.
- Allow students to page through job-hunting books or to surf the Web for examples of resumés. This will give learners ideas for categories and content.

Ideas for Using This Structure in My Classroom ✎

_____

_____

_____

_____

WHAT IS IT?

What Is It? will remind you of a game that is often used in improvisational comedy. This structure, which is sure to help students think on their feet and play a bit with content, is sure to inject a little fun and laughter into a lesson and encourage students to take small risks in front of the group.

Directions

- Begin by placing an object in front of the room and asking the group, "What is it?"
- Then encourage students to come forward and transform the object into something related to class content. He or she can tell the others what they are doing and how they are using the object, or that person can be more secretive about their performance and students can yell out guesses. The only rule is that the students must wait for the learner on stage to set the object down before another person can take a turn.
- Remind the group that only one student should approach at a time to act out a scene.
- To follow up on the content, you might give additional information about the scenes performed or ask students to identify factual problems with the scenes.

Example

A high school history teacher presented a roll of paper towels to his class and told students they would be playing *What Is It?* as a review game. The students were, therefore, charged with using the towels in ways that would help all of them recall the content studied during the Civil War unit. The teacher first gave the students a chance to page through their textbooks for ideas and to brainstorm in groups of three. Then he called for volunteers. The first student came up, unrolled some of the toweling and pretended to read the Emancipation Proclamation off the long "pages." The next student put the towel roll on his head to represent Abe Lincoln's stovepipe hat and pretended to be visiting a camp to shake hands with soldiers in Antietam. The teacher followed the humorous portrayals of Lincoln with a summary of some of the former president's political beliefs.

Methods to Maximize Engagement and Participation

- Invite students to form small groups and, after a few moments of planning time, ask each group to come to the front of the room to act out a scene using the prop. This will be particularly helpful if some students are nonverbal or have limited movement.
- Show the object and have students brainstorm ideas for transforming the object with a partner before they are asked to come up and perform individually.

- For a student with reading learning disabilities or any student who needs practice in reading for content or comprehension, the sequence of this structure can be altered slightly. Provide time for the particular student to read a related text chapter on the subject of concern, and highlight key concepts and important vocabulary. The same student then reads these highlighted elements to the class. Individual class members or the class as a whole can be challenged to scramble and search the room for objects that can be used to represent the important concepts presented.

Ideas for Using This Structure in My Classroom ✐

_____

_____

_____

_____

_____

_____

_____

_____

_____

_____

_____

_____

WE ALL OWN THE PROBLEM

We All Own the Problem (Davidson & Schniedewind, 1998) is a group problem-solving process that enables individuals to consider real issues and understand the experiences of others. This structure helps teachers cultivate a sense of shared experience and responsibility, and it promotes the development of constructive solutions to issues that have been exposed.

Directions

- This structure requires every student to anonymously respond on a piece of paper to a question, situation, or problem statement (e.g., describe a recent situation that made you feel excluded).
- After students write their statement or situation, put them into small groups of four to six (or in a large group if time allows), and instruct them to fold their papers and place them in the center of the table. Papers can be placed in a container to provide more anonymity.
- Tell each student to then draw a paper that is not his or her own, read it, and think about potential responses.
- Then, one at a time, ask students to read the problem they are holding as if it were their own and spend one minute talking about how it could be addressed.
- Following each student's reading, tell students they should open the discussion for two additional minutes to generate new ideas.
- Afterward, have participants discuss how they felt about the process, what ideas they felt were useful, ways they might use the process in other settings, or other issues that could be discussed in future sessions.

Examples

- In one middle school, this structure was used by teachers, administrators, and guidance counselors to create a forum for students to bring forward personal experiences on the themes of school safety, harassment, fair discipline, and other related issues.
- This framework was used by a teaching team in seventh grade to bring together a thoughtful group of peers who were willing to problem solve about issues related to the inclusion of fellow classmates. The teaching team generated real issues and had them prepared for students to randomly select. For example:
  - Angela wasn't included in the seventh-grade talent show. She didn't even know about it. Nobody thought she had a talent. How could we change this?
  - Sarah sits alone at a table at lunch with an aide. Other students avoid that table, and she seems kind of lonely. How could we change this?

  After generating solutions, the team of students was supported by the adults to act on their own ideas.

Methods to Maximize Engagement and Participation

- This structure as designed requires a spontaneous response by students to novel information. Many students with emotional or learning disabilities have difficulty generating ideas on the spot. The timing and pacing of the activity can be altered to maximize participation. For instance, the theme of the problem-solving session could be provided in advance; students could generate their own thoughts on the issue the night before or dictate them to a peer or adult in advance of the session.

- A student who may have trouble generating ideas for the problems could be assigned to select and read the issues, then pick a fellow classmate to respond to each problem. Reading and communication goals then become the central emphasis of the activity for this student.

- Assistive technology should also be considered to support student participation. For instance, a student with significant multiple disabilities might use a single switch and tape player to record the issues developed by her classmates. Activating the tape recorder with the switch, each issue could be played out loud in a small group. Another piece of available technology is the All-Turn-It Spinner (see Figure 1.2). Photos of all the students in the room can be placed on the template, and the student with disabilities can use a switch to spin the device, thereby randomly selecting a student to respond to the issue presented.

Figure 1.2   All-Turn-It Spinner

Source: Image courtesy of AbleNet, Inc.

Ideas for Using This Structure in My Classroom ✐

_____

_____

_____

_____

_____

_____

_____

_____

_____

_____

_____

_____

_____

_____

_____

PASS THE COMPLIMENT

Even after being out of high school for 10, 20, or even 50 years, most adults remember being teased, ridiculed, or insulted as children or as teenagers. For many, this experience (and low-level violence) is part of what it means to grow up and be a kid. Teachers, however, have the power to change that culture and inspire a different kind of name calling and labeling in classrooms.

Directions

- *Pass the Compliment* (Loomans & Kolberg, 1993) is like the old telephone game many have played at childhood parties. Ask students if they know the game and, if some of them do, ask one or two individuals to briefly explain the structure. Then tell the students that they will play a version of this game.
- Begin by instructing them all to think of a compliment they would like to pay to the person sitting directly behind them (or next to them, or in front of them).
- The first person in the row begins the game by turning around and whispering a compliment to the second person in line ("I think you are creative").
- The second person in line then turns to the third person in line and repeats the first two compliments ("I think you are creative and funny").
- The third person in line turns to the fourth person in line and shares all three compliments and so on.
- When the compliments get to the end of the line, the teacher calls on those in the back row to relay all of the compliments from the entire row ("I think you are creative, funny, independent, a good cartoonist, and gutsy").
- Row members then let everyone know if the message got through or if some of it got lost in the process.

Example

A fourth-grade teacher ended Friday afternoons with this community-building exercise. Students would sit in small circles and pass compliments around the circle until everyone had given and received one compliment. Compliments related to appearance (e.g., "I like your hair") were forbidden, as were those that were too general (as determined by the small groups of students themselves; e.g., "I think you are nice"). In addition, students were encouraged to use a compliment that was specific to that particular week (e.g., "Your oral report was really outrageous and inventive—I loved it").

Another Version of This Activity ☼

Pick one or two students at the end or beginning of the day or week and have five classmates give them a compliment. Compliments can be general or teachers can ask students to focus on something specific. For instance, a middle-school teacher might read a student's story and ask his or her classmates to provide five compliments related to the story ("a creative title," "a surprise ending," "the part on the staircase was really suspenseful," "good use of adjectives," "a lot of great detail in the description of the golf course").

Methods to Maximize Participation and Engagement

- Help all students learn what a compliment is, what it sounds like, and what a good compliment includes. Some learners simply do not have practice sharing this type of information. For extra practice, begin or end the day or the class period by asking students to give group compliments ("We created amazing poetry this week").
- Bring in the school psychologist or social worker to coteach this activity. Some students (particularly those with autism, emotional struggles, or certain learning disabilities) may be receiving counseling or support to enhance their social skills. Involving other professionals can help students understand that cooperation and collaboration are schoolwide issues.
- Create a "thanks for the compliment" poster or chart that hangs in the classroom at all times. On this poster, list words and phrases that are often used in compliments (e.g., "You are really good at _____"; "You always have great ideas for _____"). Seeing this language will not only help students who struggle to think of ideas for meaningful compliments but it may also help students with emotional difficulties (and others) to remember to stay positive, be reflective, and be kind to each other.

Ideas for Using This Structure in My Classroom ✎

_____

_____

_____

_____

_____

_____

_____

TWO TRUTHS AND A LIE

Two Truths and a Lie (Bennett, Rolheiser, & Stevahn, 1991; Sapon-Shevin, 1999) is fun and energizing and can be integrated into the classroom as a get-to-know-you activity, a weekly exercise in creativity and collaboration, a curriculum preview or review, or a way to immerse students in content. To encourage conversations that may be in some way related to curriculum, teachers can ask students to be general or to focus on specific topics for the exercise. For instance, students can be asked to share two truths and a lie related to the Nile River, the ocean, percussion instruments, or triangles.

Directions

- Instruct students to simply write three statements on a slip of paper. Two of them are truths, and one of them must be a lie (see Figure 1.3).
- Then have learners get into pairs or into small groups, read their statements, and ask their classmates to guess which statements are lies and which are truths.
- If time permits, have students share short stories related to their truths and lies.

Examples

- A third-grade teacher who had many students from a local homeless shelter in her classroom used this exercise several times throughout the year to encourage students to share information about themselves and to learn about others in the classroom. Because she was always gaining and losing students throughout the year as families moved in and out of the shelter, she found that this activity gave all of her students opportunities to get to know each other better and gave new students, in particular, opportunities to share something positive and interesting about themselves even though they had missed the getting-to-know-you activities in September. This creative teacher also used the activity to challenge her students academically and socially. When one of her learners was reluctant to try something new or to take a risk, she would whisper and remind them that the new learning or opportunity could be listed as one of their new truths in *Two Truths and a Lie* if they went through with the task or challenge. For instance, when one of her students refused to try simple stunts on the balance beam in physical education, she reminded him that he could boast about being a gymnast if he took the risk on the beam. Another student was encouraged to enter a local art contest when the teacher reminded her that she could call herself a "local artist" in the next game of *Two Truths and a Lie* because her painting was on display at a neighborhood coffee shop.
- A high school art teacher asked students to choose an American artist to study for an end-of-the-year project. As a fun way to encourage research, she asked students to do a quick computer search of their assigned artist

Figure 1.3   Two Truths and a Lie Worksheet

Name _____

Two Truths and a Lie

Write one "fact" in each box. Two of the "facts" should be true and one should be false.

```
┌─────────────────────────────────────────────────────────────┐
│ #1                                                           │
│                                                              │
│                                                              │
│                                                              │
│                                                              │
│                                                              │
│                                                              │
└─────────────────────────────────────────────────────────────┘


┌─────────────────────────────────────────────────────────────┐
│ #2                                                           │
│                                                              │
│                                                              │
│                                                              │
│                                                              │
│                                                              │
│                                                              │
└─────────────────────────────────────────────────────────────┘


┌─────────────────────────────────────────────────────────────┐
│ #3                                                           │
│                                                              │
│                                                              │
│                                                              │
│                                                              │
│                                                              │
│                                                              │
└─────────────────────────────────────────────────────────────┘
```

and then write two truths and one lie about the person. One student, Marc, was assigned Jackson Pollock and wrote, "He was a major force in the abstract expressionist movement," "His style of art is known as Cubism," and "One of his influences was Diego Rivera." Then in small groups, students played *Two Truths and a Lie* and three of the students in Marc's group correctly indicated that Pollock was not a cubist. The teacher pointed out that the exercise not only got students to start their research immediately, but also gave them some introduction to or review of artists they would not be studying in great detail.

Another Version of This Activity ✿

Have students write three facts about themselves that they think others do not know or will not be able to guess. Then put all of the slips in a hat and have students draw them out one by one and guess who wrote each fact. After a few guesses are made, the author raises a hand or otherwise reveals himself or herself.

Methods to Maximize Engagement and Participation

- If you use this several times during the year, students may enjoy trying different prompts. For instance, you might ask students to share one truth, one lie, and one wish.

- In some cases, it may help to give students time to brainstorm about their lives. Give them specific ideas to explore such as "What are five things you have accomplished?" or "Name three of the riskiest things you have tried," or "What is one thing that makes your family unique?" This will give those who have difficulty thinking on their feet options for their three submissions.

- Due to communication challenges, memory issues, or other learning difficulties, some students may have a hard time coming up with three things to share. These students might be encouraged to work with family members to write their three "facts" or they might complete the *Two Truths and a Lie* worksheet with a teacher or speech and language therapist who can help and give direct instruction in determining the difference between truths and lies.

Ideas for Using This Structure in My Classroom ✎

_____

_____

_____

_____

_____

IT'S A SMALL WORLD

Students will most likely be familiar with the expression, "It's a small world." In this activity, they will have an opportunity to see what a small world it is in their own classroom. This team-building exercise asks students to think about characteristics that make them unique and those that bind them to others in the class.

This structure is an especially useful one to use in schools that are working to introduce students with certain differences to others in the group. For instance, if the school has recently welcomed several students from another school (e.g., boundary changes, building closings), students with disabilities, students from a certain cultural group, or students who have not previously worked together in the past (e.g., multiage rooms), this activity can be used to help students make instant connections with one another.

Directions

- To begin the activity, ask students to find a partner. With that partner, they should make a list of at least five things that they have in common with one another, such as
  - their favorite dessert,
  - the month of their birthdays,
  - the number of siblings they have,
  - the color of the socks they are wearing,
  - their favorite restaurant, or
  - anything else the two of them can generate.
- Once the pairs have completed their first list, they should split up and wander around the room looking for someone else who shares at least one list item with them. Students then sit down with this partner and generate five new items of commonality.
- Have students repeat this exercise once or twice so they are able to create lists with most of the other students in the class.
- When students are finished working with several partners, ask them to come back to their own seats and discuss their learning from the exercise:
  - What did you learn about your classmates?
  - What did you learn about yourself?
  - What did you learn about our community?

Example

A fourth-grade teacher used this activity on the first day of school so that all of her students would learn more about one another. Although most of them had been educated together in the small school for at least three years by the time they arrived in her classroom, some of the students were completely new to the school because of the district's new plan to close down a segregated special education school and move students with disabilities into the same school as their neighbors, siblings, and same-age peers. During the activity, many students who thought they knew each other realized there was a lot they didn't know about the classmates they had been educated with for several years. Likewise, they learned they had a lot in common with the students with disabilities they were meeting for the first time. For instance, Richard, a boy with cerebral palsy, and his new classmate, Raul, realized that they both had spent time in a hospital (Raul for appendicitis and Richard for surgery on his back); both had three siblings; both had been born in Mexico; and both had the same favorite toy, which was the video game system, Xbox.

Methods to Maximize Engagement and Participation

- If some of the students are not familiar with the expression "It's a small world," explain it to them and ask certain students to share "small-world moments" they have experienced.
- Provide possible categories for students who might struggle to generate ideas on their own. Use Figure 1.4 or generate your own categories and copy them for some of the students or for all of them.
- Walk around the room and help pairs who are stuck; share new category ideas or prompt them to eavesdrop on other groups for help. Some students who have significant speech and language or pragmatic communication issues may need the teacher to model the question-and-answer exchange that should occur between students to uncover similarities. For example, the teacher would lead the interchange by saying: "Mindy, I noticed that you like horseback riding. Ask Julie in this way: 'Julie, I like to ride horses, do you?'" In addition, the teacher can use her own knowledge of experiences at school that two or more students share to ensure that learners are recalling shared events as a source of similarity. For example, the teacher might recall aloud that six students in the classroom attended the school ski trip together.

Ideas for Using This Structure in My Classroom ✐

_____

_____

_____

_____

_____

_____

_____

_____

_____

_____

Figure 1.4   It's a Small World Worksheet

Name _____

It's a Small World

Fill in the blanks with a partner. You can write your answers or draw pictures to represent the answers, or you can both write the answers and draw pictures. When you have the same answer in one of the categories, put a checkmark (✓) in the right column.

Name: _____		**Name:** _____		✓ **here if the answers match**
favorite dessert		favorite dessert		
favorite color		favorite color		
type of shoe I'm wearing		type of shoe I'm wearing		
birthday month		birthday month		
favorite restaurant		favorite restaurant		
state I was born in		state I was born in		
number of siblings I have		number of siblings I have		
_____ _____		_____ _____		

MAKIN' MOTTOS

Many groups have mantras, themes, slogans, or mottos that bind members together and advertise or promote their common purpose. In this activity, students learn about and create their own mottos as a way to build community and articulate a shared vision or belief.

Directions

- Begin by asking students to discuss what a motto is and why groups or individuals use them (e.g., to promote unity, to promote the beliefs of a group). Then share that you will be asking small groups of students to create their own mottos to represent their values, beliefs, or purposes in learning.
- To assist students in their brainstorming, share some mottos of well-known groups. For instance:
  o "Be Prepared" (Girl Scouts)
  o "Serve One Another" (Red Cross)
  o "Always Faithful" (U.S. Marines)
  o "Character, Courage, and Loyalty" (Little League)
- Individuals or teams then present their motto to the group, and discussion can take place as necessary. You can be specific about precisely what the motto must represent or leave the task more open, depending on the goals or objectives of your lesson or of your classroom.
- Classroom content can even be tied into this activity. Students may be charged with creating a motto for a literary character or for a historical figure, for instance.

Implementation Tip ✋

Because it will be fairly easy for students to come up with a motto in a short period of time, you may want to teach students how to brainstorm and require that they do so for a given period of time before selecting their motto from the list of suggestions. Remind students that "anything goes" in brainstorming and that the goal is to generate a long list (not the perfect answer) in this stage of the process.

Examples

- A seventh-grade social studies teacher used mottos in the beginning of the year to help students come together as learning teams. He asked them to create mottos that would represent their views on learning history. Group creations ranged from the humorous "Learn It and You Might Win on a Game Show" to the more serious "History . . . Important to Look Back Before Moving Forward." He used the activity again to have students think critically about content. During a unit on World War II, he assigned a different country to each team and asked each group to generate a potential motto for their nation. He asked students to come up with several options in a period of 30 minutes, and students then chose the one that best represented the essence of that country's struggle, attitude, and actions during the late 1930s and early 1940s. The team assigned the United States generated the motto, "Making the World Safe for Democracy . . . Again!," and the German team came up with the slogan, "A Global Germany."

- During their unit on communities, a third-grade class generated mottos for their small cooperative groups. Then they made elaborate banners featuring their mottos and hung them around the classroom. Tiala, a student with significant motor difficulties, could not contribute to the banner activity as her physical challenges made drawing nearly impossible. In this group, the students worked together to create images for their banner (see Figure 1.5) using Microsoft's PowerPoint presentation software. Changing the materials for this group allowed Tiala to select images with her switch, make decisions about the placement of those images, and work on her individual goals of independently turning on the computer and typing her name to sign into a program.

Figure 1.5   Making Banners Using Microsoft PowerPoint Presentations

Methods to Maximize Engagement and Participation

- As a way of preparing for the activity, ask students to make a list of ideas for which they personally stand or of their values and beliefs. If certain students need assistance with this kind of abstract thinking, assign this portion as homework, and ask those learners to discuss the list with their parents or other family members.
- Let students do an Internet search for mottos so they get a sense of how different groups are able to communicate their values or their mission in just a few words; you might encourage students to search for their state motto or the motto of religious, recreational, or political groups that are

popular in their communities or of groups they care about personally
(e.g., gay and lesbian support groups, cultural organizations).

• Have students look up *motto* in the dictionary to get a more concrete
sense of the word and concept.

Ideas for Using This Structure in My Classroom ✏

_____

_____

_____

_____

_____

_____

_____

_____

_____

_____

_____

_____

_____

ONE STEP AHEAD

One Step Ahead is a visual assessment of students and their beliefs, attitudes, knowledge, or ideas. It is also a helpful way to get "all voices on the table" without asking for verbal communication. For this reason, this structure can be a nice way to encourage participation if one or more of the students in the classroom are nonverbal or have communication that is not reliable.

Directions

- Ask all members of the class to stand in a line at one end of the classroom.
- Make a statement about a belief, an idea, an attitude, or some piece of knowledge that learners may possess. Students are instructed to move "one step ahead" if they can respond affirmatively to the statement or if it is true for or about them. For example, if the teacher says "I am female," then all of the girls in the classroom should move forward one step and all of the boys should stay at the starting line.
- Once all first moves have been made, the teacher will make another statement. Again, students will move forward if the statement is true for or about them. Possible statements include
  - I am the oldest child in my family,
  - I am 12 years old,
  - I have a pet,
  - I am wearing blue jeans, and
  - I am a vegetarian.
- Statements can also be related to class content such as
  - I can name all of the planets,
  - My favorite character in *To Kill a Mockingbird* is Scout,
  - I was born in the Midwest, and
  - I can name a track and field event.
- When the first student or students cross the finish line, the class can discuss some of the answers and responses to the statements.

Example

A high school geometry teacher used *One Step Ahead* to as a review for a semester exam. All prompts were related to class content:

- I know the difference between a right angle and an acute angle,
- I know the Pythagorean Theorem,
- I can bisect an angle,
- I can define *ray*,
- I can find the area of a parallelogram,
- I know what *geometry* means, and
- I can name a geometry-related career.

Throughout the activity, the teacher called on individual students to share their answers and to teach mini-lessons to the rest of the group. When only three students stepped forward and claimed to know the Pythagorean Theorem, he called those three to the front of the room, had everyone sit down on the floor wherever they were on the "grid," had the students reteach the concept at the board, and then asked everyone to stand and respond to the "I know the Pythagorean Theorem" prompt again, waited for everyone to step forward, and resumed the game.

The actual prompts were written by a fellow student who had been out of class for several weeks due to a serious illness. The student's first assignment on returning to the classroom was to review the chapters he had missed and then develop some questions related to the unfamiliar content. In assigning this role, the teacher created a nonthreatening and enjoyable way for the young man to immerse himself back into his studies while giving him opportunities to get some support from his peers.

Methods to Maximize Engagement and Participation

- List the statements on the board if some students need visual support. Or, to get students involved before the activity begins, allow all students to list possible prompts on the board and choose from this list during the activity.
- Vary the prompts so that students with different types of knowledge and expertise might have opportunities to share and move. For instance, you might have several prompts related to content (e.g., I know the difference between ___ and ___; I can name three facts related to _____) and several others related to effort, attitude, or individualized goals (e.g., I learned more than I thought I would; I met my individual goals for this unit; I could have worked harder yesterday).
- Give students a moment to "turn and talk" about the prompt with a partner near them before asking them to move. This way, students are able to ask and answer questions (particularly helpful if some learners are confused about a prompt) and give individual responses during a whole-class activity.

Ideas for Using This Structure in My Classroom ✐

_____

_____

_____

_____

_____

_____

_____

ONCE UPON A TIME

Everyone loves a good yarn! This storytelling activity is a fun way for students to experiment with new concepts, ideas, and words. It can also be used as a writing exercise to help students with creative thinking. Furthermore, it can help learners with sequencing, creating details and descriptive language, and developing story openings and endings.

Directions

- Begin this activity by listing several categories on the board. For instance
  - favorite book characters,
  - animals,
  - students in the class,
  - things you might get as a gift,
  - party games, and
  - common household chores.
- After generating the list, ask students to suggest items that would fit into the categories, and write those responses on the board as well. For instance, in the "favorite book characters" category, students might name Scrooge, Goldilocks, and Harry Potter.
- The group is then charged with integrating those ideas or items into a story.
- Begin the story with, "Once upon a time . . ." and call on a student to fill in the next line or two. The object of the game is to incorporate as many of the items as possible from those generated in the classroom list. Therefore, a student drawing on the aforementioned categories might finish the teacher's sentence with "Scrooge was playing pin-the-tail-on-the-donkey when he saw a beautiful girl across the room."
- Inform students that they must contribute only one sentence at a time. The story moves around the classroom until everyone has contributed at least one sentence, then the teacher can choose to end the story or move around the classroom once or twice again.

Examples

- After teaching about avoiding colloquial language or trite expressions in their work, an expository writing teacher broke students into four small groups and gave each a tape recorder. She then told them they could invent a story about anything, but they had to incorporate at least a dozen trite expressions into the tale. She started the students out with this sentence, "I was working like a dog, feeling happy as a lark, when I saw John walking across the court, looking so angry there was fire in his eyes . . ."
- A fifth-grade teacher, interested to know what facts her students had picked up during their ongoing study of the United States, asked students to tell a collective story integrating the following elements:
  - a U.S. river,
  - a symbol of the United States (e.g., eagle, flag, Statue of Liberty),

o a state in the Midwest,

o a famous American landmark, and

o a U.S. president.

To add an extra level of challenge, some students with strong abilities in language and expression were told they would have to insert a simile, a metaphor, or an example of onomatopoeia as they took their turns in the exercise.

Methods to Maximize Engagement and Participation

- Many cultures have a long tradition of passing stories down through the generations using storytelling. In some cases, master storytellers use gestures and vary their voice quality as a way of enhancing the story. To interest kinesthetic learners, consider introducing gestures and other storytelling methods and allowing students to use them as they engage in this activity.
- To make the activity more challenging for students needing enrichment, the teacher can choose to add requirements to the task, such as "by the end of the story, you must have"
  o included at least four vocabulary words from this unit,
  o shared at least three learnings from the last chapter, or
  o integrated three facts from yesterday's lecture.
- Allow some students, if necessary, to use alternative forms of communication to participate. For instance, some students may want to use some type of pantomime during their turn. Others may need to hold up picture cards that represent people, events, or ideas. If such an adaptation is necessary, the others in the group must work together to interpret the idea and add it into the story.
- After generating the list of concepts, stop the activity momentarily and give all learners time to collect their thoughts and to jot down some ideas on paper. Some students may even need a "cheat sheet" with possible responses for each category listed.
- If one of the students in the classroom has significant cognitive disabilities or communication struggles, you could have this learner participate by choosing a story-starter card from a group of three or more. Each card might contain a phrase that could be injected anywhere into the story (e.g., "and then something unexpected happened"). Others could be used to start the story (e.g., "Once upon a time, there was a strange little man . . ."). The cards can be illustrated and can be constructed by other learners or by the teacher.

Ideas for Using This Structure in My Classroom ✎

_____

_____

_____

_____

Teaching and Learning 2

 WALK IT TO KNOW IT

Although teachers routinely use bulletin boards, easels, and of course, the chalkboard for displaying important information, they often forget the untapped canvas of the classroom floor! The entrance of the classroom, the path from the door to students' desks, and even the tiles underneath student desks can feature images, words, or concepts that will promote student learning. Teachers might make charts to teach any number of concepts, including the scientific method, steps to solving a binomial equation, or the parts of a business plan. This structure is especially helpful for visual and kinesthetic learners.

Directions

- To prepare for this structure, you (or your students) will need to design flow charts (⇨□⇨□ ⇨□ ⇨□ ⇨□) or series-of-events chains on paper and then transfer each square to a separate piece of poster board or butcher paper.
- The squares are then laid out on the classroom floor in a pattern that will help you communicate the concepts. If the content you are teaching is a chronology of events (such as the timeline of the Crusades), the pattern will likely be a straight line, but if the content is a cycle (such as the carbon cycle), the paper can be arranged in a circle or in any other shape that will help the learner understand and remember the concepts.
- As students enter the classroom each day or during a lesson where the concepts are introduced, have all of the students stand and walk through the sequence.
- Have students explain each step as they walk over it, or simply have them read the information on the board or paper aloud. You might have students trod over the chart one time or several times over the period of a week or month.

Examples

- A fifth-grade teacher used *Walk It to Know It* to help her students remember significant events in the American civil rights movement. Every day when students came through the door, they were required to step on each one of the squares in sequence and read each aloud (see Figure 2.1).

Figure 2.1   Walk It to Know It Timeline Example

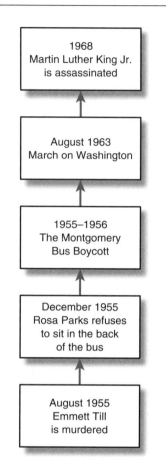

- A ninth-grade health teacher used this technique to teach her students the steps used in CPR. The first day it was introduced, the entire class spent 20 minutes moving through the steps repeatedly. For the rest of the year, the teacher asked students to enter her classroom by stepping individually on each mat. Furthermore, she assigned a short movement to each step of the process and occasionally asked students to step on the mats and act out each of the steps using the actions she had shared with them. For Step 1, which is to call out to the person, she had students wave their hands and yell, "Are you OK? Are you OK?" During class, she periodically quizzed students on the steps to be sure they were retaining the information.

Methods to Maximize Engagement and Participation

- Ask students to chant the words on each square as they step on them. This will help some learners retain the information more effectively.
- Let students hop or skip through the sequence. Adding this extra bit of movement can give some students an opportunity to release energy in a constructive way. As in the CPR example, students might also be taught motions that relate to different steps and asked to use these motions or engage in actions as they move through the sequence.

- As a way to help students remember the sequence even better, ask individual learners to help in the construction of the flowchart, or ask small groups of students to construct their own *Walk It to Know It* charts and have them take turns trying out all of the different versions. Students can print the text on the computer or write it by hand and embellish the floor mats with clip art, photographs, or drawings.

Ideas for Using This Structure in My Classroom 🖊

_____

_____

_____

_____

_____

_____

_____

_____

_____

_____

_____

_____

_____

_____

FISHBOWL TAG

Fishbowl (Silberman, 1996) is a discussion tool that brings students into a public forum to converse about topics of interest. In traditional formats of *Fishbowl*, students are gathered in two concentric circles. The inner circle is the discussion circle, and the outer circle is the listening circle. Usually, the teacher provides selected questions for the discussion circle to address. The listening circle offers observations and additional comments at the end of the inner circle's dialogue. After a period of time, the inner and outer circles change places.

Fishbowl Tag is traditional *Fishbowl* amplified! This version picks up the pace and makes the process into a good-natured interchange of positions and ideas that will keep all students moving and thinking.

Directions

- Arrange a small inner circle of five to eight students. Create a second concentric circle of the same number. The remaining students look on as the audience from their seats.
- Compose several open-ended questions or issues that will serve as a springboard for discussion. Toss the questions into a hat that students or the teacher will draw from or, to add meaning to the metaphor, the questions can be drawn from a real fishbowl.
- Someone from the inner circle then draws and reads a question. The inner circle responds spontaneously to the question, sharing personal knowledge and opinions.
- This is where the fun begins! The inner-circle players may leave their chairs only after contributing an idea to the discussion. At that point, they can leave the inner circle and tag someone in the outer circle to replace them. The teacher or the student leaving the inner circle then tags a student in the larger audience to fill the seat in the outer circle.
- Inner-circle members may be replaced in another way. If they have already spoken in the inner circle, a savvy observer from the outer circle who has a stake in the discussion can enter the inner circle and tag that member, thereby replacing them.
- Continue the discussion and game of tag continues for a designated amount of time.

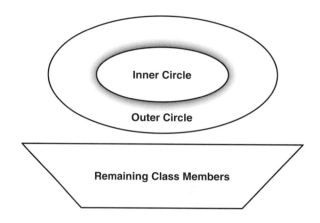

- At the end of the discussion, the instructor might note key summary points or ask for comments from the observing class members.

Implementation Tip ✋

In the first trials of this structure, students will not be used to interacting with one another face to face in a circle. They will look to and want to direct their comments at the teacher for affirmation or next steps. It is important to define your role at the beginning of the process, and even position yourself on the periphery of the fishbowl so that the students focus on one another. The only reason for the instructor to intercede is if significant misconceptions need to be rectified or if the dynamics of the dialogue become unproductive.

Examples

- A high school English teacher used this structure as a method to guide students through key novels. Questions were developed that prompted analysis of the text at certain points. All students were given time to respond to the questions individually in writing before being placed in the *Fishbowl Tag* formation. For example,
  - How does the author use organization, details, and imagery to define the narrator's attitude toward the characters?
  - Consider the mention of historical events in the text and the time period in which the text was written. What events taking place in the world at this time might be influencing the author?
- In a first-grade classroom, this structure was used as a forum for community problem solving when student disagreements erupted or when classroom relationships were stressed in some way. The prompts varied based on the specific issues that had occurred, such as
  - Some students have noticed that their belongings, snacks, or lunches have been missing. What can we do as a classroom community about this?

This same classroom teacher used this format to solicit positive events in her students' lives and reinforce optimistic thinking through open-ended questions such as

  - One thing I like about our classroom is . . .
  - I hope that . . .
  - One good thing that happened to me recently is . . .
  - I'm grateful that . . .
  - I wish . . .

Methods to Maximize Engagement and Participation

- Strategically select the most talkative students to begin in the audience; this will assure that the game of tag will be advanced by those who have strong opinions.
- Let a student act as "Tag Master." This person does not have to enter the discussion circle but instead energizes and surprises the group (and usually inspires laughter) by tagging and replacing discussion members

randomly. Equip this person with a child's plastic fishing pole to "reel in" participants to add to the entertainment.

- To advance students' communication skills, the teacher can assess positive behaviors exhibited by students during the *Fishbowl* that facilitate a productive debate. Figure 2.2 is a rubric that outlines potential communication behaviors that students should exhibit and also those from which they should refrain during the *Fishbowl*. The teacher can keep a running log by marking a student's initial next to the behaviors observed to provide feedback after the session. Middle and high school students can be encouraged to use this form as observers and provide constructive feedback to their peers.

- To ensure attentive listening by the remaining class members (those acting as the general audience), give them a critical observation task. See Figure 2.3 for a sample guided notes outline that can be used to provide feedback to the discussants and debrief the overall experience.

Figure 2.2 *Fishbowl Tag:* Score Sheet

Name _____

Productive Discussion Actions	Student Initials	Less-Than-Productive Actions	Student Initials
Taking a position on a question; paying attention		Not paying attention	
Making a relevant comment		Making irrelevant comments	
Using evidence to support a position		Making points that are not supported with facts	
Leaving space for another person or bringing him or her into the discussion		Monopolizing the discussion	
Acknowledging another person's statement		Attacking someone personally	
Asking a clarifying question		Asking questions that are irrelevant to or disconnected from the discussion	
Moving the discussion along		Interrupting	

Figure 2.3 *Fishbowl Tag:* Notes and Questions

Name: _____

What did you hear in the discussion that was important?

_____

_____

_____

_____

_____

Did you have a point that didn't get presented? What was it?

_____

_____

_____

_____

_____

Who do you think was most convincing, or presented their point particularly well? What did they say or do that was convincing?

_____

_____

_____

_____

_____

What new questions were raised for you as you listened to the discussion?

_____

_____

_____

_____

_____

_____

- Some students may find the structure itself difficult to understand and learn. One way to ease anxiety and focus attention on the prompts is to ask all students to silently practice the movements related to the structure before giving them any content to discuss. Have learners walk through the tagging movements and the transitions between circles without having to observe a real discussion.

- If some students on the outside need help to leap into the fray, the teacher can act as coach by walking around the perimeter of the audience and (via whispers or Post-it Notes) giving students tips for making relevant contributions. He or she may even want to provide some students with cue cards that feature lesson-related facts or ideas so the individual will have something appropriate and on target to share.

Ideas for Using This Structure in My Classroom ✎

CAROUSEL

This structure provides an efficient way to give students opportunities to report on their work without using a lot of class time. *Carousel* is an entertaining way to have students generate and share information with one another. Furthermore, as students move from group to group and teach material to one another, the idea that knowledge resides within the learning community (not just with the teacher) is continuously reinforced.

Directions

- Assign students to work in small groups. Then assign each of the groups a number.
- Give the groups a task. You can give them a problem to solve, questions to answer, an issue to discuss, or a project to complete.
- After giving the students time to collaborate and complete the task, tell the groups they must assign one member of each group to be a visitor. This individual will rotate to an adjoining team and share the work he or she completed with the original group.
- The students should move systematically through the groups based on their assigned numbers. Therefore, if the visitor is a member of Group 1, he or she moves to Group 2 and so on. The visitor from the group with the highest number moves to Group 1.
- When the visitor arrives, he or she shares with this new team the original group's discussion, results, or outcomes.
- After giving the visitor several minutes to share this information, the teacher again rotates the visitors and the process begins again in a new group.

Examples

- A high school drama teacher put students into groups of four and asked them to write a monologue, titled "My Life," based on their experiences as teenagers at the turn of the century. They had to keep in mind the elements of a powerful monologue they learned in class (e.g., personal emotion, having a point), and each person had to contribute at least three ideas. When students were finished writing, they selected one person to perform the monologue during a *Carousel*-style rotation. Each visitor, therefore, performed for each of the five groups in the class.
- A second-grade teacher used *Carousel* to give students practice in creating compound words. Each group was responsible for creating a poster of various compound words (e.g., swimsuit, lunchbox) complete with illustrations. The visitors then toured the different groups sharing their posters. Frieda, a child with cerebral palsy, had limited communication and was learning to use a new augmentative communication tool, the BIGmack switch (see Figure 2.4). She was, therefore, assigned to be a visitor so she could share her poster and have six opportunities to narrate it. At each

Figure 2.4   BIGmack Switch

Source: Image courtesy of AbleNet, Inc.

station, she would hit her switch to activate a 60-second message that explained the poster and was recorded by students in her small group.

Methods to Maximize Engagement and Participation

- Give students who benefit from repetition the job of visitor. If a learner is working on reading fluency, for instance, the teacher might assign the visitor the task of reading a poem, story, script, or list during the rotations.
- If a student identified as the visitor cannot easily summarize and share knowledge from his or her group, he or she might be given a graphic organizer or a cheat sheet of key points to use during the initial group's discussion and for each rotation. Students with more significant physical disabilities or communication struggles might even be taught to tape record the discussion of their original group and share this tape with subsequent groups.
- Have all of the visitors bring some product (e.g., photo, drawing, chart, poster) with them to illustrate or represent the work accomplished by their group; this will enhance the visitor's presentation and make his or her teaching multisensory, which will in turn help the visual and hands-on learners who will be taught by the visitor.

Ideas for Using This Structure in My Classroom ✐

_____

_____

_____

_____

NOVICE OR VETERAN?

This structure provides a method for differentiation when there is a clear discrepancy in the class between students who are more experienced and students who are less experienced with a topic or concept. Students who self-identify as novices on a topic have the opportunity to explore multisensory and multilevel materials to learn more about the topic, whereas students who identify themselves as veterans on the topic must formulate a fact or example to illustrate the concept. Members of the veteran group must join their separate pieces of information into a coherent mini-lecture that is then delivered to the rest of the class. Novices generate questions from their individual study of the topic to ask (or stump!) the veterans.

Directions

- It is critical the teacher emphasize that we are all both novices and veterans. Our position of novice or veteran is dynamic and will change with different topics or skills. For example, you may be a veteran regarding molecular biology but a novice in ballroom dancing.
- At the start of a new topic or unit of instruction, do an assessment or ask students to self-assess their level of knowledge or experience with the key concepts. Create two groups representing novices and veterans on the topic.
- Those who have identified themselves as veterans write down something they already know and can teach others about the topic on a note card.
- Students who are novices write down or generate one question on the topic, which is recorded on a note card. For this piece of the lesson, you will want to provide multilevel and multisensory materials to the group (e.g., photographs, videos, reference materials, different leveled texts). Students can then use these materials to inspire their questions and the upcoming discussion.
- While novices are exploring and reviewing materials, the veterans come together to share, validate, and integrate their separate pieces of information. The veterans' goal by the end of the class period is to mesh their individual knowledge into a mini-presentation for the rest of the class.
- When the veterans present, the novices have the opportunity to ask their questions. Questions that can't be answered sufficiently by the veterans are marked as a priority for instruction by the teacher during the unit.

Implementation Tip ✍

To begin this activity the teacher should clearly explain the difference between a novice and a veteran: A veteran has past experience with the concept and feels he or she knows something on the topic that can be taught to others. A novice has less experience with the concept and would like to know more about the topic. It is important to emphasize that everyone will have the opportunity to be a novice or veteran at some point during the year.

Example

In a second- and third-grade multiage classroom in which the teacher taught the same students for two years, the novice and veteran structure was used during a science unit on the life cycle and behavior of butterflies. The teacher of this classroom focused the unit on monarchs each year. The students who were currently third graders had experienced learning activities about this topic the previous year. By nature of the class, the third graders were veterans on the topic, whereas the second graders were novices. The teacher employed this structure at the start of the unit that focused on curricular science standards related to the interdependence of life. A key objective was for students to understand that an organism's patterns of behavior are related to the nature of its environment.

In this team-taught classroom, the special educator guided the third graders to recall their learning experiences from the year before, which included observing real caterpillars hatch into monarchs, releasing them, and communicating with children in Mexico to where the monarchs migrated. While the third graders prepared their presentation to explain these activities, the second graders reviewed tangible written and pictorial material about butterflies, generating questions to ask their classmates. When the novice and veteran interchange occurred, questions that could not be answered were used as points of inquiry for the entire class.

In this classroom, a second-grade student who was an English Language Learner had moved from the Baja Peninsula and had lived in an area where monarchs gathered in migration. He was part of the veteran group due to his firsthand observations of the butterflies. In addition, any of the second graders who felt they had relevant "butterfly knowledge" could self-select as veterans.

Methods to Maximize Engagement and Participation

- Before the veterans present, have them review available materials to verify their perceived knowledge.
- Allow novices to work in partnerships or small groups to generate questions.
- For students who have difficulty coming up with questions, a list of prepared questions can be provided. The students can review and highlight the ones that are most interesting to them.
- It is important to use this technique across academic and nonacademic topics so that all students have the opportunity to share an area of expertise. Teachers should avoid having the same learners functioning as veterans or novices each time the activity is used.
- Another role that might be used in this activity is that of moderator. This student could have the important role of logging all of the classroom questions and presenting them to the veterans. If the learner has speech and language difficulties, the questions could be entered into a speech output device or tape recorder. During the question-and-answer session, the student can be in charge of presenting each question of interest to the novices.

Ideas for Using This Structure in My Classroom ✐

_____

_____

_____

_____

_____

_____

_____

_____

_____

_____

_____

_____

_____

_____

_____

THE WALKING BILLBOARD

Too often in a large classroom, the same students share information day after day. This leaves many students, including those who are shy or not as confident in their responses, to participate only passively in these traditional lesson structures. An alternative to calling on individual students to share responses to a single question is to ask all students to generate an answer and then to wear it around the room as a way of advertising their thoughts.

This structure works best when you are seeking a variety of answers to a question that is open ended and has no clear right or wrong answer.

Directions

- To begin, provide every participant with a sheet of flip-chart paper and a marker. Provide a question (or a few related questions), and ask all students to write a response to that idea on the chart paper.
- Hand out two pieces of masking tape to each student, and instruct all learners to attach the chart paper to their clothing in some way; tell them they are now walking billboards.
- Instruct them to wander around the room and take in information and ideas from other billboards while being sure to give several different individuals a glimpse at their idea. The other important direction in this exercise is that there should be no talking; this is a visual and nonverbal activity designed to focus students' attention on what they see instead of what they hear.
- Give students approximately 15 minutes to wander, and then have them come back to their desks. Quiz them informally on what they saw and what their reactions are to the assorted responses.

Example

A language arts teacher, teaching students about how to write a good short story, had students write responses to the prompt, "In a good short story, you will always find _____." Students then had five minutes to develop a response on a piece of chart paper. The teacher announced to the students, "I will know you are finished when you are wearing your response," and demonstrated how she wanted them to attach the paper to their clothing. When all of the students were wearing their individual responses, the teacher put a timer on for 10 minutes and instructed the learners to mill around the classroom and read their classmates' billboards. She encouraged them to try to view as many of the responses as possible without running, shoving, or disrupting others. When students returned to their desks, the teacher then asked them to jot as many responses as they could recall on a sheet of paper. The class, as a whole, then discussed what makes a good short story.

Methods to Maximize Engagement and Participation

- During the sharing piece of the activity, allow students to share information verbally and to ask questions if some or all learners might not be able to get all the information they need from reading responses (or if some learners will struggle with reading or reading quickly).

- To pique student interest, give more time to allow learners time to embellish their billboards. Some may want to add illustrations or stickers, use stencils, or write in an artistic font. You may even want to share advertising secrets with learners as they work to make their billboard memorable. For instance, you can encourage them to use bold lettering, develop catchy slogans, or create icons or images that their classmates will easily recall.

- Photograph students as they walk around the room; these images can then be used as a fun and informal review for those who want to revisit the content and the exercise.

- Have a student function as the researcher. He or she can walk around observing the billboards and record information on a chart or on the chalkboard. This individual might also tabulate the data in some way and report the most common, the most unique, and the most notable responses to other class members via a diagram or list. This task might be appropriate for a learner needing enrichment or one who enjoys analytical tasks.

Ideas for Using This Structure in My Classroom ✎

_____

_____

_____

_____

_____

_____

_____

_____

_____

_____

_____

_____

DINNER PARTY

At some point, we have all been to a dinner party where small clusters of people form and have brief conversations. As new partygoers arrive or people naturally mingle, the groups are reconstituted, and conversations are picked up or changed midstream. This learning structure mimics these informal group interactions.

Dinner Party is a technique that facilitates the sharing of information among multiple students in a short period of time and can be used as an alternative to whole-class question and answer.

Directions

- Devise a number of topics or questions to which each individual will formulate a response.
- Present the first question or topic, and call a number between 2 and 6. At this point, everyone is expected to stand, shuffle around the room, and gather in a group of people based on the number you have called (i.e., if the number 2 is called, students would form partnerships). Students quickly share their ideas in the group in a round robin format.
- After a few moments, present a new topic or question, and call a different number. Students must then switch groups and find new class members with whom to interact.
- After several rounds, you might ask students to share ideas that they heard in their small groups.
- Ways to debrief include asking students:
  - What was the most interesting thing you heard?
  - Did you find common themes in people's responses?
  - Identify one idea that challenged your thinking.
  - What is one thing you learned?

> ### Implementation Tip 🖐
>
> Provide more involved and complex questions for smaller groups (e.g., groups of two or three), and devise short-answer questions as the groups are increased in size.

Examples

- In an introduction to a unit on probability and statistics, a teacher formulated questions like the following for *Dinner Party* discussions:
  - What are some ways that data are collected?
  - Have you ever questioned the results of a poll or survey? Why or why not?
  - Share one way you have seen statistics used in everyday life.
- A middle-school instrumental music teacher used *Dinner Party* to help students teach and learn about jazz. He began by playing a piece of

music by John Coltrane and asking students to form their first group. He then presented the following questions:

o What do you hear?

o What might the artist be communicating with this song?

He gave the students a few moments to discuss, then had them switch groups and put on a piece of music by Dizzy Gillespie and repeated the questions. During the course of a 50-minute class, he asked students to repeat this exercise using music from Billie Holiday, Etta James, and Thelonious Monk.

Methods to Maximize Engagement and Participation

- Some students (particularly those with language learning disabilities or students who are English Language Learners) may find it difficult to respond to unexpected and fast-paced questions. Providing the questions ahead of time so that a verbal or written answer can be formulated may be helpful. These answers can then be carried and used as a guide during the group discussions.
- The whole class may benefit from advanced review of the questions if they are unfamiliar with the premise of this learning structure. While the class is reviewing the questions silently, some students might rehearse their answers briefly with a teacher, a therapist, or even another student.
- If some students struggle to find partners during the transitions of the activity, you may want to facilitate some of the groupings by wandering around and helping students get into the appropriate-sized constellation. To make even more purposeful partnerships, you can take this forward by assigning the groups in advance. Give each student a card that lists the name of each person they need to find for each new group. For instance:

Group 1—Find Tom, Amanda, Maia, and Kris

Group 2—Find Randy and Paul

Group 3—Find Ryn
- To make this activity even more fun and light, take the dinner party metaphor another step and serve punch or water and healthy snacks. These refreshments may wake up some of your more tired students and literally give them "food for thought."

Ideas for Using This Structure in My Classroom ✎

_____

_____

_____

_____

THE COMPANY YOU KEEP

This fast-paced and entertaining game from Mel Silberman (1996) is appropriate as a review, an icebreaker, or an introduction to new material. *The Company You Keep* can last for 30 minutes and be used to teach a lesson, or it can be used to recap the day's learning during the last five minutes of a class period. This structure allows students to learn about the perspectives and knowledge of their classmates and gives participants' opportunities to see interests, ideas, and even values they share with one another.

Directions

- To prepare for this game, make a list of questions that are appropriate for teaching or reviewing content, and give students an opportunity to make a controlled choice. In other words, the question should have limited answers. Examples include the following:
  - Do you agree or disagree with capital punishment?
  - Do you or do you not understand how to measure angles?
  - Who is your favorite character from *The Color Purple*?
  - What Spanish-speaking nation would you most like to visit?
- Then, clear some space in the classroom or move students to a hallway.
- Call out a question, and ask students to mill around the classroom looking for all others who have the same answer they do. Therefore, students who agree with capital punishment would cluster together and those who disagree would do the same. If the prompt contains multiple responses, the teacher should tell students to cluster together with their small group and to make sure they move away from other groups so all discrete groups can be identified.
- When students have formed groups, have them shake hands with the "company they keep." Then do some debriefing with the class. You might ask students to teach each other about the category they chose or to explain why they chose what they did. For example, if you had students choose their favorite character from a book, you can call on them to defend their choice and ask students in other groups to interrogate this choice and ask clarifying questions.

Implementation Tip 🖐

You may want to ask students to sit down together or to link arms once groups have formed, so all participants can clearly see what and where the different groups are. For further clarification, students might even be asked to hold up signs indicating the name or identity of their group.

Examples

- When a fifth-grade class was studying regions (e.g., Northwest, Midwest) of the United States, the teacher asked them to respond to the following prompts and find the "company they keep":
  o region in which I was born,
  o region I would most like to visit,
  o region that has or appears to have the best tourist attractions,
  o region that seems the most beautiful, and
  o region that seems to have the most important natural resources.

To prepare for this exercise, the teacher asked the students to review the information in their textbooks on these particular issues (e.g., natural resources, tourism) so they would be able to give thoughtful, evidence-based reasons for making choices.

- During a unit focused on *Of Mice and Men*, a high school English teacher asked students to find the "company they keep" for the following prompts:
  o the character in the book they most respected,
  o the character in the book they felt was the most misunderstood,
  o the character in the book they felt was the weakest, and
  o the character in the book they felt was the most sympathetic.

As students met with each new group, they discussed why they chose the character and what specific evidence from the book drove their decision. Students needing a bit more support in identifying and remembering character traits and motivations were given an index card with short descriptions of the major characters (e.g., "Lennie is George's companion. He is a big, strong, and gentle man. He has disabilities and his speech is slow. Lennie dreams of owning a country home where he can raise rabbits and share a simple life with George").

Methods to Maximize Engagement and Participation

- Some students may need to see or be told the various choices for sub-categories. For example, if the teacher asks students to identify the continent they would most like to visit, and some students don't know any of the continents, that learner will need some preteaching to generate a response.
- Write the prompts on the board or overhead so that students can hear and see choices, or give certain students an index card with this information on it so they can have a reminder of the task and the prompts as they mill around the room.
- To make the activity slightly more challenging (and to create built-in supports for English Language Learners), ask the students to find "their company" without speaking. This way, students have to be very creative in locating others in their group.

- Once students are in their respective groups, call on individual students to defend or explain why they chose as they did. Vary questions to suit the needs and abilities of each student. You might ask very concrete questions of some learners (e.g., "Why do you like George?") and very complex questions of other students (e.g., "Who or what does George symbolize?").

Ideas for Using This Structure in My Classroom

_____

_____

_____

_____

_____

_____

_____

_____

_____

_____

_____

_____

_____

CLASSIFY, CATEGORIZE, AND ORGANIZE

This structure promotes learning by discovery and problem solving and holds students responsible for making sense of key information and conveying it to the class. It also helps students see the connections between separate pieces of information and take an active role in conveying relevant concepts alongside the teacher. Often, students will make teaching points that the instructor had intended to present. This process promotes greater spontaneity in instruction and ensures instructional time is not spent directly teaching what students already know or could discover.

Directions

- Create note cards, strips of paper, or actual pictures related to concepts that can be classified, categorized, or ordered in two or more groups (e.g., different species of animals or words that are different parts of grammar, such as nouns and verbs).
- Give each student in the class one card (or paper slip or picture) that will fit into at least one category or group. Then encourage students to move around the room viewing each other's cards to find others who can form a group that is related in some way.
- When students believe they have classified themselves correctly, give the group a short amount of time to identify its category and determine how the different parts of information each person holds are related. Each group should then be asked to report its newly integrated findings to the class. The group members may also add novel or additional information they know about the concept that is not represented on their cards.
- After each group presents, the teacher can use the information to reinforce key points, clear up misconceptions, or provide more elaborate explanations.

Implementation Tip ✍

To simplify the task for your students and to save on time, you can provide the categories to the class at the start of the activity (e.g., "You all have a country written on your card. You are looking for students with countries that are on the same continent as your country").

Examples

- A librarian at an elementary school used this technique to teach students different genres of books. She gave each student an actual book and asked them to look at the title and read the book description. Students had to group themselves by genres of their assigned book (e.g., mystery, suspense, horror, drama, science fiction, etc.).

- A first-grade teacher used this structure to teach animal classifications (e.g., what characteristics are associated with birds, reptiles, mammals, amphibians, and fish). For Jeremy, a student with Down syndrome and moderate intellectual disabilities, participation in this activity focused on language and reading goals. His key objective was to identify the picture of a snake and read the words *scaly skin* from his card loudly enough to be heard by others in the class. Other students in the room had to determine whether Jeremy fit their animal category.

- A fourth-grade general and special educator teaching team created cards that constituted a number of different equations. When put together correctly, a correct solution was evident. Here is a sample of the cards developed: 2, 10, (×), 15, 12, (−), 13, (=), 120, (=). When students correctly configured themselves in two groups of four these equations were formed: $10 \times 12 = 120$ and $15 - 13 = 2$. The teachers could differentiate easily by creating cards (and ultimately equations) that ranged in difficulty level. Some student groups could form algebraic equations, others could make fractions, and still others could represent the process of addition or subtraction.

Methods to Maximize Engagement and Participation

- If a student does not yet have skills to accurately associate his or her card information to a category, directly teach the student what information to be looking for. For example, "You have an owl on your card. An owl is a bird. You should look for other people who have birds on their cards." If even this is too complex, you could change the objective of the activity completely and ask the learner to simply find a match to his or her card. In this scenario, you would need two identical owl cards, and you would give the student the task of finding another owl; the two students would then need to find their *Classify, Categorize, and Organize* group together.

- Give one student the name of the unifying category on a separate colored card; others must come to him or her to form a logical group. This adaptation might be especially helpful for students needing extra support, as these students do not have the responsibility of finding a group; instead, students find them. These cards might also contain extra information about the topic or group (e.g., "Because an amphibian's skin lacks a shell, scales, or outer drier covering, most amphibians live in wet or damp situations to prevent dehydration") so the student holding that card shares information (and serves in an expert role) with the group, once it is assembled.

- Mix up the form of information given to different students. Some information on the cards may be in single words, others are short phrases, and others are only in picture form.

- Strategically give a card to a student that contains content that he or she knows well and can associate to others.

Ideas for Using This Structure in My Classroom ✐

_____

_____

_____

_____

_____

_____

_____

_____

_____

_____

_____

_____

_____

_____

COLLECTIVE BRAINWRITING

This technique illustrates the adage "two heads are better than one" as students generate solutions to multiple issues posed at the same time by classmates in small problem-solving groups. Depending on the topics used, this strategy can be either high energy or relatively quiet and low-key and can, therefore, be adjusted to meet the needs of students and to meet the requirements of the task.

Directions

- Place students in groups ranging in size from 4 to 10. Direct each person in the group to think of an issue or problem to be solved and summarize it in writing on a half-sheet of paper.
- When they are finished writing, tell students to place papers in the middle of the table.
- Students should then be asked to take a paper that is not his or her own, read the problem silently, and write at least one responsive idea on the bottom half of the paper.
- When students complete this step, ask them to return these papers to the center of the table and again choose a new one (or pass all papers to the left). On this second sheet, students should add new ideas to the responses of the previous writer.
- Continue this exchange for an agreed-on time limit.
- At the conclusion of the activity, have learners retrieve their original papers, review the proposed ideas, and, when appropriate, select one or more solutions to implement.

Examples

- After studying the effects of various forms of pollution and earth-friendly solutions, students were asked to pose environmental problems to one another. Two such questions were, "How can we reduce urban storm water runoff pollution?" and "How can we reduce air pollutants from car exhaust?" Based on research done during the environmental unit, examples of solutions generated by students to the first question included
  - Don't pour oil or grease into a trash bin, storm drain, the street, or a sanitary sewer, or on the ground; and
  - Don't use toxic chemicals like bleach and detergents to clean trash containers outside.

  A student with less-developed writing skills was able to represent his solutions through pictures and short phrases.

- This activity provides a safe forum for students to bring forward sensitive issues that may be occurring in their school lives. A homeroom teacher, therefore, asked students to respond to prompts related to their school community and personal lives such as, "Describe a situation in which you felt peer pressure." Students were then charged with responding with encouragement or suggestions. The teacher also occasionally kept the activity open and gave no prompt, encouraging students to identify anything that might be troubling to them.

Methods to Maximize Engagement and Participation

- Students often need practice writing their problem statement with enough specificity to allow a reader to understand the situation. Consequently, an additional step can be added by allowing each person to briefly describe his or her problem before placing written summaries into the center of the table.
- Some students may feel very anxious about sharing problems and ideas of this nature with their classmates. You can attempt to minimize this discomfort by asking students to set ground rules before starting the activity. For instance, you could ask students to be reinforcing to one another and to share positive comments (e.g., "These ideas are really helpful").
- For students with handwriting difficulty, attempting to keep up with the problem exchange could be challenging. The use of assistive technology writing aides such as the portable computer companion keyboards by AlphaSmart (see Figure 2.5) could allow a student to keep pace with classmates by typing responses.

Figure 2.5   Neo AlphaSmart Laptop

Source: Photo courtesy of Renaissance Learning, Inc.

Ideas for Using This Structure in My Classroom ✐

_____

_____

_____

_____

_____

PROFESSOR PARAGRAPH

Professor Paragraph allows all learners in the classroom to become experts for the day. It is often useful when students are studying for an upcoming quiz or test or when the text is very challenging. It can also boost comprehension of the text, in that this strategy can help students read more carefully, identify pieces of the text they understand and those they do not, and engage in multiple readings of key passages.

Directions

- Instruct students to briefly review the content in a small section (one to three pages) of their textbook or of any other reading selection (e.g., newspaper, Web page).
- Ask them to find a paragraph they understand and could explain to somebody else.
- Instruct students to write this paragraph in their own words (paraphrase) and copy this new version onto an index card.
- When all students have prepared their index card, ask students to stand and find a partner. Give them two to three minutes to teach their paragraph to their partner and to have their partner teach his or her paragraph to them. When the teacher says, "new partners," the students scramble to find a new partner and repeat the lesson with the new partner.
- You can have students can change partners once, twice, or several times.

Example

A U.S. history teacher used *Professor Paragraph* to teach the U.S. Constitution. Because the document is very long and (to many learners) quite dry, he felt the structure would give students a chance to have a little fun with the content while also giving them opportunities to interpret the text and translate it into contemporary language. Although many of the students chose the same pieces of text to teach (e.g., the Preamble), the teacher viewed the student-to-student interactions as a great opportunity for learners to get multiple interpretations of the document and to, therefore, begin to understand why it is a document that is forever being argued about, theorized about, and discussed by individuals, professors, scholars, and even lawyers, judges, and the president.

Two students with learning disabilities were in this classroom. One worked with a teacher to prepare his card. The teacher, acting as a scribe, wrote down the student's responses as the young man shared them verbally. The other student chose to paraphrase his paragraph as homework the night before.

Methods to Maximize Engagement and Participation

- Some learners with language and communication difficulties may need to create their card in advance. Still other learners may need a peer to help them construct their card.

- If many students have difficulties with writing and paraphrasing, you can photocopy the text and allow some students to select and cut out the paragraph they will be sharing. To engage in the paraphrasing step of the activity, allow these learners to highlight key words or passages and underline the most important part of the selection.

- For extra challenge and to boost understanding for some, you can suggest or even require that students illustrate their paragraph. This extra assignment can be beneficial in several different ways; it will create interest for artistic and visual students, and it can enhance comprehension for many others, as asking students to draw a complex concept requires them to not only understand the concept they are representing but also consider how to help others understand the concept visually. Students might even be taught specific visual mapping symbols (Margulies & Maal, 2001) to represent concepts on their cards. These symbols could be taught to and practiced by all students so learners can quickly and efficiently share information (see Figure 2.6 for examples of symbols that might be adopted in a science class).

Figure 2.6   Possible Visual Mapping Symbols

Ideas for Using This Structure in My Classroom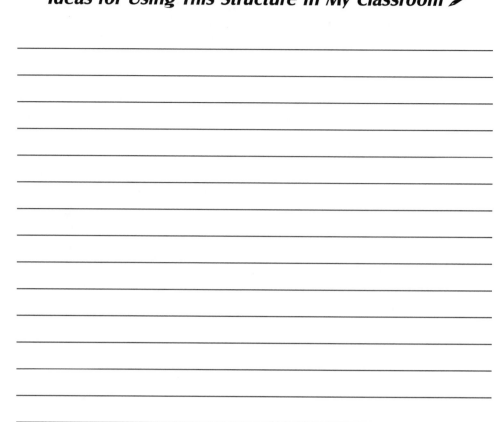

_____

_____

_____

_____

_____

_____

_____

_____

_____

_____

_____

_____

_____

_____

Studying and Reviewing 3

 MOVING TO THE MUSIC

This activity is great for Monday mornings and Friday afternoons alike. In other words, it can be used either to wake up a tired classroom or to engage excited and energetic students (who might be thinking more about the 3:00 bell than course content) in learning. All you need to engage in *Moving to the Music* is some popular music and a few questions that can be used for discussion or brainstorming.

Directions

- Begin by giving students small slips of paper or index cards with four (or any other number that you choose) questions on them. These four questions will be used as discussion points during the activity, and their corresponding numbers will indicate how many partners they will find for that particular question. For instance, they will find one partner for Question 1 and two partners for Question 2.
- To start the movement piece of the activity, turn on the music and ask students to begin milling around the room. Tell them they must keep moving and that, at this point in the activity, talking is not permitted.
- After a few moments, turn the music off. This serves as a cue for students to find a discussion group. For the first "music break," students will look for one partner and discuss the first question on their card. For the second "music break," students will look for two partners and discuss the second question on their card and so on.
- After students have answered all four questions during four different breaks, bring them back together as a class and debrief the activity. You might ask them to share ideas they themselves generated or offer ideas they heard from others.

> ### Implementation Tip ✋
>
> You may want to give students some guidelines on how to manage the time given. For instance, if you are going to give them five minutes to discuss each question, they might want to roughly divide the number of minutes by the number of participants and assign that much time to each individual. Or you might be even more directive and time the intervals for them, announcing "switch" every time a new person should begin answering the question.

Examples

- A third-grade teacher used this activity at the beginning of the year to learn about the math skills and abilities of his new students. His prompts were as follows:

  1. One strategy I use for addition is . . .
  2. One strategy I use for subtraction is . . .
  3. When I don't know the answer to a problem, I . . .
  4. When it comes to math, I could use help with . . .

- A creative-writing teacher often used *Moving to the Music* to get her students to generate new ideas and to give them new and different ways to get feedback from other writers on ideas they might be developing. One day, to push students into starting a new story, she gave them the topic of "a bank robber" and used the following prompts:

  1. Describe her.
  2. Share at least three details about her past.
  3. Describe the bank she will rob.
  4. What is one plot twist you can envision in this story?

  Following the exercise, the teacher had the students go back to their desks immediately and start writing. She asked them to write without "thinking, stopping, editing, or evaluating" for at least 20 minutes.

  Occasionally, she involved herself directly in the activity. Each time she used *Moving to the Music*, she put a star (☆) next to a question or prompt on a few students' cards. This indicated to these learners that during that particular formation, they needed to find the teacher and include her in that group. This was her way of hearing from individual students and allowed her to give and get information and engage in mini-assessments. She used it, in particular, to challenge students but also to check in, in particular, with two students with learning disabilities who found it difficult to think on their feet and often got frustrated with brainstorming.

Methods to Maximize Engagement and Participation

- Choose music that students will enjoy or that they might find interesting, or if certain students seem disengaged or disinterested in the activity, you might ask them to choose the music that will be used.

- You can differentiate instruction by giving different students different assignments on their index cards. That is, not all students need to have the same questions or the same assignments. For example, on any one of the four exchanges, most of the students might be directed to share a strategy or idea, whereas a few others may have directions on their card to meet with the teacher (as in our example), check a resource (e.g., go to the dictionary to find information), practice a skill targeted in an Individualized Education Plan, or do some observing of other groups.

- To draw in your kinesthetic learners, ask students to dance or move in a certain way during the transitions. A teacher who happened to be teaching about Egypt, for instance, asked all students to "walk like Egyptians" as they toured the room. She added to the fun by playing *shaabi*, popular contemporary music of the country.

Ideas for Using This Structure in My Classroom ✏

_____

_____

_____

_____

_____

_____

_____

_____

_____

_____

_____

_____

_____

_____

POPCORN

Popcorn is controlled chaos at its best. We have so named it because during transitions, students fly around the room in random directions. *Popcorn* is useful for the times when you want students to share information, teach and learn from each other, and get ideas or opinions from more than one person in a very short period of time. It is the perfect choice for lessons that lend themselves to lots of conversation, questioning, and chatter.

Directions

- Begin by instructing students to get "knee to knee, face to face" with one person (this can be done on the floor, standing, or with two chairs).
- Then have them decide on roles for the activity; one person must be stationary for the entire activity. The other person must be mobile and will have opportunities to move about during the activity.
- When you give the first prompt (e.g., "Tell everything you know about Greece"; "Share some tools that are used to measure"), the stationary students will answer and keep talking until you say "switch." During this time, the mobile students are not allowed to speak at all.
- When you say "switch," the mobile person begins talking, answering the same question. At this time, the stationary students should not be speaking and should only be listening.
- After a few minutes, yell out "popcorn"; when students hear this, they should abruptly stop speaking, and the mobile students should get up and find an empty chair (or empty spot if you are not using chairs) across from another stationary person.
- The process then begins again. When you give the next prompt, the stationary students answer first (again). (The stationary students will always answer first.)
- It is very important to reinforce that students who are listening should *not* speak. They should be silent while their partner shares.

> ### Implementation Tip ✋
>
> Ask students to spread out at the beginning of this activity. Have students scattered as far apart as possible to make milling around and switching chairs easier.

Examples

- An American history teacher used this structure to give learners opportunities to learn from one another and to see the divergence of opinion even in a small class. She asked students, who were studying suffrage, the following questions:
  - Does voting matter in a democracy? Why or why not?
  - Why do you think some men did not want women to vote?
  - Why do you think some women did not want the right to vote?

o What risks did the suffragists take?

o Who are the heroes and heroines of the suffrage movement?

- A sixth-grade teacher used *Popcorn* to review elements of teamwork with her students. She asked students to answer the following questions in their pairings:

  o What does it mean to be a team player?

  o What does collaboration mean to you?

  o What does negotiation mean to you?

  o How can you be encouraging to your teammates (be specific)?

  o What talents do you bring to a team?

- After the pairs shared their thoughts on each one of the questions, the teacher brought the students back into a whole-class formation and asked them to share some of the things they heard from their classmates. They then drafted a set of guidelines for working in teams that they would use for the entire school year.

  J.P., a student with autism, who became very anxious during this activity, created his own adaptation by asking to be stationary and to meet with his partner in the hallway. Another student, who had a hearing impairment, made the same request. Therefore, when students made their switches, they knew they had to scan not only the classroom but also the space outside the room as they looked for new partners.

Methods to Maximize Engagement and Participation

- Have students who need more help thinking of a quick response be the mobile partner; this way they will always get to hear their partner give an idea before they are required to do so.
- Give the prompt, and then give a minute of think time so that both partners have time to formulate thoughts.
- Some students may feel uncomfortable with this much movement and activity. You might want to allow some of your students to switch partners less frequently or not at all.
- Be sure to allow your most active learners to be mobile; this will give them teacher-sanctioned opportunities to move.
- If necessary, allow some students to wander around the classroom and listen to conversations before joining in the activity. This role, eavesdropper, can be added to the structure for one round or for the entire activity. Or you can have several students serve as eavesdroppers for the purpose of collecting data on student learning or to observe and encourage the collaborative behaviors of classmates.

Ideas for Using This Structure in My Classroom ✎

_____

_____

_____

TOSS-A-QUESTION

For an informal and fun way to have students exchange ideas and take responsibility for teaching one another, try *Toss-a-Question* (Kagan, 1990). In this structure, students get to ask and answer questions, teach and learn, and share expertise with classmates. Plus, they get to make paper airplanes without being reprimanded! This structure not only works as a tool for reinforcing content, it is also a quick way to lighten the classroom mood.

Directions

- Begin by giving each student a sheet of paper (or see Figure 3.1 for a worksheet that can be used), and remind them to put their names at the top.
- Then tell students to fold the papers in half and label one half "question" and one half "answer."
- Then give them a few minutes to generate a question related to some recently covered content.
- Tell the students that you will know they have finished writing their question when you see that they have crushed their paper into a ball (or folded it into an airplane).
- When all students are finished writing, tell them to "toss a question." They should toss their paper across the room (being careful not to hit another student).
- Then, when the commotion clears, students are invited to pick up a question, unfold it, and begin working on generating a response. Give students a few minutes to work on the task and then ask them to crush their paper into a ball again.
- Once again, have them toss their papers into the air and retrieve another from the floor. This time, their task is to check the work of the first recipient and add any other information that might help the questioner.
- At this point, if the question is fact based, you may want to allow students to use textbooks or other materials to ensure that students are sharing accurate information.
- Finally, have students toss the questions back to their authors.
- Individual students can then be called on to share their questions and answers.

Implementation Tip ✋

If you don't want the commotion and chaos of papers flying through the air, this activity can be carried out in a more controlled (albeit less exciting) fashion by having students toss all of their questions into a garbage can or large bowl and then retrieve one from the same spot, or by having students make eye contact with one other person and gently exchange papers via a short person-to-person toss.

Figure 3.1   Toss-a-Question Worksheet

Toss-a-Question

Name of Question Writer _____

Name of Answer Writer _____

Question:

Answer:

Examples

- Students in an eleventh-grade English class were asked to toss discussion questions related to the novel they were studying, *Night*, by Elie Wiesel. Questions included, "How did Wiesel survive such adversity?," "What does the title of this book mean?," and "Wiesel writes often of fathers and sons. Why is this an important theme in the book?" Students tossed their complex questions twice, and the teacher gave the recipients more than 10 minutes to attempt an answer. Students then tossed the questions a third time, and that recipient filled in missing information, added details, or offered another opinion.

- In a fourth-grade classroom in Massachusetts, students were studying their home state. The teacher had students ask and answer questions about their favorite things in the state. The questions were to be open ended and were not to be based on facts but on student preferences. As an example, she shared the question, "What is your favorite tourist attraction in Massachusetts?" and tossed it to a student who volunteered that she loved going to the Freedom Trail, an attraction that focused on historical sites relevant to the American Revolution. That student then tossed the question to another student who also had to answer the question. Students had their questions tossed around the room five times and then returned to them as a piece of data they could use in upcoming reports on the region.

Methods to Maximize Engagement and Participation

- If particular students will struggle to write their own question on the paper, they might be provided a set of prewritten questions on Post-it Notes. Their task is to read the questions and choose one for the exercise. The Post-it can then be stuck on the paper. If writing is not a problem, you could also provide the students a list of potential questions and allow them to copy their question on to the sheet.

- Once the papers are tossed, let students work in partners to answer their respective questions; this may ensure accuracy and may inspire more thoughtful answers.

- To challenge particular students, the teacher can get in on the game. Create enrichment questions that are especially difficult and identify certain students who will receive their "toss" from the teacher.

Another Version of This Activity ✿

Instead of using questions and answers, have students work on a piece of collective work through this structure. For instance, a middle-school language arts teacher had students write a collective poem by asking one learner to write a line and then toss it to another student, who would add a line and toss it again. Stories, fact sheets, brainstorming lists, essays, sheet music, drawings, and many other products can be constructed in this way.

Ideas for Using This Structure in My Classroom ✎

_____

_____

_____

_____

_____

_____

_____

_____

_____

_____

_____

_____

_____

_____

GUESS WHO?

Students playing *Guess Who?* will learn to be savvy about the content as well as problem-solving skills such as questioning and deduction. Although this game takes some up-front planning, once cards are constructed and the rules are known to the students, the exercise can be repeated several times.

Directions

- Create a set of index cards with names, concepts, ideas, or definitions written on them. For example, a geometry teacher might create a deck of cards with a different shape on each (e.g., rhombus, right angle).
- A card is then taped to each student's back (or forehead if you want to be a bit silly) showing everyone, except the person wearing the card, what is written on it.
- The player with the card on his or her forehead (who does not know the name on the card) must then ask closed questions (requiring only yes or no answers) to establish his or her identity. Using the same geometry example as before, a student might first ask the question, "Am I a triangle?" or "Do I have straight lines?"
- This structure, although often used for amusement alone, can help students think in complex ways about course content. Figuring out one's identity in this game requires critical thinking and attention to detail. If you are trying to figure out your shape, for instance, you need to determine what elements in particular separate different types of shapes (e.g., tools used to draw them, lines or lack thereof, types of angles involved if any); this type of categorization can enhance students' comprehension of a particular concept.

Implementation Tip ✋

If the set of ideas or concepts you have assembled is particularly challenging, consider showing all of the students all of the cards before handing out individual cards to individual students. This way, the game will run more smoothly as learners guess options from a field they have already reviewed.

Examples

- One high school chemistry teacher used this game during a lesson on the periodic table. Each student had one element taped to his or her back and had to ask questions such as, "Am I a solid?," "Am I a liquid?," "Am I heavy?," "Am I inert?," and "Are the letters of my symbol part of my name?" Roy, one student in the classroom who needed extra challenge during this unit, was responsible for moving around the room and helping struggling students come up with good questions to narrow the field of possibilities. When one student was stumped and could not guess his element, Roy came up with the questions, "Am I used for nuclear fission?" and "Does my element begin with a P?" When the student got yes answers to the questions, he was able to correctly guess that the element was plutonium.

- A tenth-grade English teacher used *Who Is It?* to help students learn and remember the characters in *The Great Gatsby*. To provide each student with a unique label and to make the activity more challenging, she included story characters (e.g., Gatsby, Daisy), story symbols (e.g., flowers, ashes), and story ideas (e.g., nouveau riche) in the game. The teacher made a slight adaptation in the activity for Sinead, a young woman with cognitive disabilities in the classroom. The students played the game twice (once when they were halfway through the novel and once when they were finished), and both times, Sinead knew that the teacher would assign her a character (not a symbol or an idea). Sinead worked with a peer to review character traits and descriptions on a few different occasions and rehearsed a few questions in advance with a paraprofessional in the classroom. She was, therefore, able to guess her character both times by using simple questions such as "Am I a male or female?," "Do I die?," and "Am I rich?"

Methods to Maximize Engagement and Participation

- Pair pictures with words on the cards for students who may be struggling readers.
- Some students may need a "starter" set of questions for the activity; give those learners a few key questions to use as they begin the exercise (e.g., "Am I a person, place, or thing?").
- Ask students to generate the packet of cards that will be used in the activity. You can assign this as an enrichment activity for students needing more challenge, or you can ask all students to work with a partner and generate two cards to add to the classroom stack.
- Give a "sponge" activity to students who guess their identity early in the activity. Instruct students to sit down immediately and write down at least three things they learned from the questions and answers provided.
- Consider adding additional roles to the activity; some students can walk around the room giving hints to the askers and answerers, and others can simply observe and record information that is passed from person to person.

Ideas for Using This Structure in My Classroom 🖊

_____

_____

_____

_____

HOT SEAT

Hot Seat provides a fast-paced way to engage a whole class in skill or information drills. It also can be used for gathering information from each member of the class in an efficient manner that promotes face-to-face interaction. In addition, because this structure requires students to work with several different partners, *Hot Seat* is a great "get-to-know-you" activity for the first day of class and at other key points in the school year.

Directions

- Position students in two rows (with these rows facing one another). Inform students that one row will act as the interrogators (or *questioners* if you prefer a more friendly term) and the other row will act as the informants and sit in the "hot seats" (because they will be questioned by each of the interrogators).
- To get the activity started, the interrogators are given (or they are asked to generate) a question. Each interrogator, however, must have a different question.
- The questioning round begins, and each interrogator asks his or her partner in the hot seat the question.
- The informant has a few moments to answer before the teacher announces "next seat." At this point, the person in the hot seat moves down one chair and sits across from a new interrogator. Thus, the interrogator asks the same question to a new partner at each rotation.
- After one full round of questions, interrogators change positions and become informants. Questions can remain the same or be changed for the second round.

Implementation Tip ✋

This structure can be particularly beneficial for students who need multiple trials to learn or memorize information. Place these students in the interrogator seats first, so they are able to read the question repeated times and hear answers from numerous classmates.

Examples

- A high school biology teacher used this technique to review content that had been missed on an exam. Each student reviewed his or her exam individually and created a question-and-answer card for any incorrect item. The cards from every student were distributed to the interrogators. Therefore, at some point in the rotation, each person heard and responded to the question card that he or she developed.

- Several elementary school teachers used this technique to teach data collection and graphing using information gathered about class members' preferences. Each interrogator developed a question that allowed multiple responses (e.g., "What is your favorite color?"). During the activity, then, each interrogator was given a graph to chart the responses of each person who sat in the hot seat. At the end of the activity, data had been gathered and graphed on at least 10 different questions. The class analyzed the data together to determine high and low frequency responses by the class.

Another Version of This Activity ☼

Rather than having the students in the hot seat rotate, the questions used by the interrogators can be passed down the row so that each pair receives new information to ask about and answer.

Methods to Maximize Engagement and Participation

- The teacher or students can develop the questions used by the interrogators, or you can structure the activity so that learners answer some teacher-created questions and a few of their own. After a few rounds of teacher-generated questions, tell students they need to generate a related question for each informant.
- Students who may need more practice with the information can remain in the position of interrogators.
- For students whose goal is mastery of specific content, smaller rows of interrogators and hot seat sitters can be formed to review selected information. Therefore, in a classroom of 24 students, instead of having one row of 12 and another row of 12, you could have two *Hot Seat* rotations going on at the same time with two rows of 6 working on one side of the room and two rows of 6 working on the other side of the room.

Ideas for Using This Structure in My Classroom ✐

_____

_____

_____

_____

_____

_____

_____

SAY SOMETHING

Short, Harste, and Burke (1996) developed this shared reading strategy, which promotes comprehension and construction of meaning from text. Students read a piece of text together, then at key points, they stop and exchange thoughts about what has been read. Learners are encouraged to look for relationships between new information and their existing knowledge.

This active reading structure can be particularly helpful for students who have comprehension difficulties and for students who are unable or unlikely to read material outside of class. Allowing in-class reading assures that all students are on the "same page," so to speak, regarding the content.

Directions

- Select a piece of text that ranges in length from a few sentences to a few pages.
- Place students in pairs, and give each learner the reading selection.
- Tell students they will be reading the text as a team. Direct them to glance at the text and decide the place in the text they will stop and "say something" to one another. Tell them they may share a question that comes to mind, make a point, connect the information to personal experience, note something that was particularly interesting, or paraphrase what was read.
- Ask them to begin reading. Remind them to repeat the process of stopping, sharing, and starting until they finish the selection.
- After all pairs have completed the selection, a whole-group discussion can be facilitated.

Implementation Tip ✋

When teaching students to engage in this strategy, it may be necessary to demonstrate the process for students and develop a list or menu of different ways to say something. The instructor should move around the room during the process to ensure that students remain on topic and to monitor the length of the *Say Something* interchange. The goal is to make brief comments to one another rather than launching into debate or discussion.

Examples

- In a unit comparing creationism and evolution, a high school science teacher used this technique with two short readings, one an excerpt from a religious text and the other an essay by Richard Leakey famed archeologist, to spark interest and controversy on the first day of instruction.
- Ruben was a fifth-grade student who is legally blind is also a very gifted musician. He loved talking to his music teacher about operas he attended with his family and new music he was learning on the piano.

To help Ruben share his talent with other students, his music teacher used *Say Something* in a unique way. Before the class was to attend *Peter and the Wolf*, the teacher asked students to listen to short segments of the symphony. Students were asked to pay attention to how the music portrayed the characters, the dynamics of the piece (loudness and softness), and the tempo. They were then cued to turn to a partner in the class and say something about the different elements featured in the lesson. To demonstrate how to engage in the activity, the teacher modeled the structure with Ruben. His complex answers about the composer's choices (e.g., Ruben noted that all of the characters are represented by a certain instrument) stunned classmates while helping them learn more about the play and about the collaborative structure they were using.

- A middle-school art teacher used this technique to introduce the surrealist painting styles of Frida Kahlo, Marc Chagall, and Salvador Dali. Each student pair was given a series of pictures by the artists. The teacher used a three-minute egg-timer to set a time frame for the students to study each reproduction of the artist's work. At each three-minute interval, the teacher cued the students to stop and say something to their partner. Afterward, the teacher asked students to comment on their emotional responses to the pictures, on the common or dissimilar styles of painting, and on the possible hidden messages intended by the artists.

Methods to Maximize Engagement and Participation

- As noted in the previous examples, *Say Something* can be used with non-text material. Students may be partnered with one student examining text on a topic and the other examining visual media (photos, pictures). At an agreed-on time frame (e.g., after examining the materials for three minutes), students can stop and say something.
- Students may also be paired with readings on the same topic but at different reading levels. At the stopping points, students share what they have gained from their own specific reading.
- *Say Something* can be implemented with one person in the partnership reading aloud.
- For students who read at a different pace, the student who completes the reading first can write down his or her *Say Something* comment while his or her partner completes the reading.
- Both students can keep a running list of comments and questions that have been generated and use it during the class discussion. This list can also assist the teacher in assessing student accountability.
- The teacher can prescribe the nature of the exchange between students, as was illustrated in the music example.

Ideas for Using This Structure in My Classroom

_____

_____

_____

_____

_____

_____

_____

_____

_____

_____

_____

_____

_____

_____

CRACKING THE CODE

When many of us were in school, doodling on your paper was viewed as off-task behavior or at least as a sign of inattention. Although times have changed and many teachers understand that students can pay attention and scribble at the same time, students are not usually encouraged to draw on their notes or otherwise "mark up" their papers. When teachers employ this simple strategy, however, the artist (or at least the doodle bug) in all students is rewarded. *Cracking the Code* can be used to check students' understanding of an assigned reading, directions, concepts in text, or homework problems.

Directions

- As students read a chapter or piece of text, ask them to code different sections or key points in the margins. The codes should be designed to reflect their understanding of the material. For example, codes can include
  - ○ a check mark (to signify understanding—"I get this");
  - ○ a question mark (to signify misunderstandings—"I'm not sure about this concept," "I don't understand what the author is trying to say," or "The vocabulary is confusing"); and
  - ○ an exclamation point (to signify points of interest or that the student understands the material well—"I *really* get this!" or " I'd like to talk about this point!").
- Coding can be done in pencil on worksheets, on books students own, or on copies of material.

Implementation Tip ✋

When textbooks are used, the student can code with self-stick notes. A set of these self-stick codes could be saved and used for multiple applications.

Examples

- After outlining procedures for the day and prior to engaging in a science lab, the instructor asked students to read the directions for the activities and examine each of the tasks to be completed. He asked students to use just two codes, a check mark to indicate "I understand what to do" and a question mark meaning "I'm kind of confused about this." The instructor then moved around the room silently viewing the codes. This assessment alerted him that a number of students were confused by vocabulary in Step 6 of the procedure. Consequently, he took a moment to explain that procedure in detail. He also provided assistance at this step to groups with members who registered confusion by their codes. An added benefit to this process was that after listening to verbal directions, the students had to read the lab sequence with greater attention to their own understanding of the material. As a result, the teacher noticed there were fewer misunderstandings and random questions during the instructional activity.

- A mathematics teacher used this strategy prior to a homework assignment in algebra. She asked students to preview the assigned problems and code them for understanding. She discovered that several students felt very confident in their abilities to solve a particular problem. Prior to ending class, she asked these students to demonstrate the problem while the rest of the class took notes. The homework was then reduced by one problem.

Methods to Maximize Engagement and Participation

- This technique can be used during a lecture or after the teacher has demonstrated a concept. Provide the class with wipe-boards or pieces of paper to code their understanding. At specific points, the teacher can ask for a "code of understanding." As a large group, students show their code for instant assessment by the teacher.
- *Crack the Code* can be used as a strategy for cultivating peer support. Teachers can have all students read a piece of text and code it. Based on the codes, the teacher can spontaneously put students in teaching-and-learning pairs to clarify each other's misunderstandings.
- For students with significant comprehension problems, the teacher and learner might code the text together using guided questions. For example, "In the reading, do you understand two causes of the Great Depression? Yes or no?" Additional review or teaching of specific concepts could be installed based on student responses.

Another Version of This Activity ✪

Instead of having students use codes to signify understanding, use them to encourage better note taking. Begin by having students divide their papers into four quadrants or columns. An icon should be drawn in each of the four sections:

- a light bulb (representing new ideas)
- a key (representing "key" ideas)
- a question mark (representing things that are still confusing)
- a face or stick figure (representing concepts they want to discuss with others)

As you give a lecture or facilitate a whole-class discussion, encourage students to record new information in the appropriate boxes. This structure can make it easier for some learners to identify areas of difficulty or confusion with the content.

Students can also be asked to generate additional icons to help them organize their notes and make the content more memorable.

Ideas for Using This Structure in My Classroom ✐

_____

_____

_____

_____

_____

_____

_____

_____

_____

_____

_____

_____

_____

_____

MATCH GAME

This structure requires students to interact in a structured way and assist each other in succeeding. It is the perfect antidote to dry and dull drill-and-practice exercises. It can be particularly helpful for teaching and reviewing facts, dates, vocabulary, and definitions.

Match Game gets students out of their seats and helps even the most struggling learner succeed. If that student cannot find the right answer, the answer may find him or her!

Directions

- Begin by making two groups of cards (A and B); each card in one group (A) must have a matching card in the other group (B). For instance, you might create one group of questions (A) and one group of answers (B), one group of words (A) and one group of definitions (B), or one group of incomplete sentences (A) and one group of words that complete the sentences (B).
- Every student is given one index card and told to walk around the room, talk to other students, and compare their card with the cards of their classmates.
- Students are also directed to help each other find their matches.
- Once students have found the card and the individual who matches their card, they should sit down next to that person and wait for others to find their matches. When all students have found matches, the pairs will share their match with the class.
- Pairs can simply read their cards to the others or quiz the rest of the class using the information they have learned from their match.

Implementation Tip ✋

To keep students on task after they have found their match, you might want to put related information, trivia, or "brain buster" questions on the back of the match cards. This way, students can discuss this additional content with their match while they wait for all other students to pair up.

Example

One teacher used *Match Game* to showcase the talents of one of her students, Marn, a young woman with autism, who was interested in trains. During a unit on transportation, Marn created one set of cards that contained concepts, words, and phrases related to trains. On the other set of cards, she wrote the corresponding definitions. One card, for instance, had the phrase *run-through* written on it. The definition of *run-through*, which is "a train that generally is not scheduled to pick up or reduce (set out) railcars en route," was written on another card. Students had to find matches for terms and phrases that were, in most cases, completely new to them. Students had fun learning the new lingo and were impressed with Marn's expertise in this area. According to the teacher, the game was the first time students in her classroom had to go to Marn to get help and information. This experience changed students' perceptions of their classmate, and it gave Marn the courage to share more of her specialized knowledge with others. In addition, all students became interested in the activity and were anxious to take a turn designing their own set of cards for the group.

Methods to Maximize Engagement and Participation

- Have some students participate in creating the cards. As in our example, being the author of an activity will be especially rewarding for a student who has expertise in a unique area.
- Encourage students to support each other during the game. Remind them that they can give clues to their classmates to help them find matches. You could even demonstrate how learners can give support. Show them, for instance, how to give clues (but not answers) to classmates or how to ask clarifying questions of one another.
- Color code the cards or add stylized text for some students so they can narrow down the number of individuals they need to approach as potential matches. For instance, a teacher using this structure to practice Spanish vocabulary might have all of the words in white and all of the definitions in pink. Furthermore, all of the verbs might be in italics. Therefore, a student assigned a card with the word *salta* printed on it knows that he or she needs to approach only those with pink cards who also have italicized text.

Ideas for Using This Structure in My Classroom ✐

_____

_____

_____

_____

_____

_____

_____

_____

_____

_____

_____

PAPER BAG INTERVIEWS

In today's busy standards-based classrooms, students have less time than ever before to socialize and to ask and answer questions about life both inside and outside of the school. *Paper Bag Interviews* (Gibbs, 1995) can be used regularly throughout the year to give students such opportunities. Students tend to enjoy the I-wonder-what-I'm-going-to-draw suspense and the personal nature of the activity.

Directions

- To engineer these unique interviews, write a series of questions and place them in small lunch bags or cardboard boxes.
- Put students into clusters of three to five, and hand each group one bag or box. Students then take turns drawing questions from the container and answering them. At any point, a student may decide to pass on a question and draw a new one.
- You can use this activity to give students opportunities to learn personal information about one another or to comment on different topics of study in the classroom. Questions can also give students opportunities to share personal stories and reflect on curriculum. For example, the question, "How are you most like Crazy Horse?" prompts students to disclose something about themselves while they consider information they have about this historical figure.

Example

A middle-school earth science teacher regularly used *Paper Bag Interviews* as a content review and as a way to facilitate positive working relationships in the classroom. During a unit on earthquakes, he included the following questions in his "interview bags":

- What is a tsunami?
- If someone gave you a beautiful house in an area known for earthquakes, would you make your home there? Why or why not?
- Name the three types of earthquake waves.
- How do you think city planning and building construction will change in the next 50 years in earthquake zones?
- What is one way individuals, a city, or the federal government can minimize the damage of an earthquake?
- What is the most interesting thing about earthquakes you have learned in this unit?
- Explain the difference between a focus and an epicenter.

To differentiate instruction for this activity, the teacher included a few "pink slips" in the bag. Students knew these brightly colored questions would be more challenging and abstract than the others. Any student was invited to choose a pink-slip question, but if he or she could not answer it, others in the group were allowed to try.

Methods to Maximize Engagement and Participation

- As in the previous example, color code the questions so students can make a choice based on their mood, skill level, or preference. Different colors could be used, for instance, for questions that are more personal in nature, more silly, or more serious, or they could be coded for level of difficulty.
- Put questions in the bags that relate to student interests. If a student in the group has just become an uncle, include a question about this big event. If a student is really interested in the Beatles, include a question about rock and roll in the 1960s.
- If you have some students using alternative or augmentative communication, you might add some interest to the activity if you ask all students to take turns answering questions using different types of expression including sign language, gestures, and pictures.
- If students in the classroom receive support from a speech and language therapist, *Paper Bag Interviews* would be a nice opportunity for coteaching or collaborative consultation. The therapist might work in the classroom during this activity and help all students improve skills related to turn taking and asking and answering questions.
- If you really want to be purposeful in what types of questions each student answers, you can put student names on individual questions, and as each learner draws a slip of paper, he or she reads the question to the learner who has been assigned it.

Ideas for Using This Structure in My Classroom ✐

_____

_____

_____

_____

_____

_____

_____

_____

_____

_____

_____

_____

HUMAN CONTINUUM

Human Continuum allows teachers to quickly view student opinions and perspectives. It also gives students opportunities, literally, to see where they stand on issues as compared with their peers. This structure works as a way to learn about student knowledge but can also serve as a values clarification exercise.

Directions

- Begin by showing students a five-point Likert-type scale on an overhead.
- Ask them, after giving a few minutes to think, to choose the number that best describes their position on an issue (e.g., "I understand how to multiply binomials," "I feel animal cloning is ethical"). Be sure to indicate the values for the scale. For example, if you want 1 to represent *disagree* and 2 to represent *disagree somewhat*, and so on, then post those labels on the Likert-type scale overhead or drawing, or on the wall itself.
- Next, ask students to distribute themselves along the wall and stand in the place that best corresponds to their response.
- Then randomly ask students to share their perspectives. You might ask a student on the high end of the continuum, a student on the lower end of the continuum, and a student in the middle of the continuum.

Examples

- In a middle-school history class, the teacher asked students to respond to the following statements using the human continuum; those who strongly agreed with the statement stood near the number 5, those who strongly disagreed with the statement stood by the number 1, and all others stood somewhere in between depending on their views:
  - John Adams is an American hero.
  - Colonists were justified in destroying property (during the Boston Tea Party) to gain political attention.
  - Women played an important role in the American Revolution.
  - Benedict Arnold was a traitor.
  - The American Revolution was a necessary war.

  As students made their choices and shuffled into line in their appropriate spots, the teacher called on individuals to share the rationale for their choices. When he found two or more learners with strong feelings at the opposite ends of the continuum, he asked them to engage in a short, friendly debate in front of the class.
- In a fifth-grade classroom, the teacher used *Human Continuum* as a way to kick off a unit on nutrition; she told the students they would use the exercise as a way to assess their knowledge, behavior, and beliefs and as a way to compare their lifestyle and habits with others their own age. She asked students to respond to the following prompts:
  - I eat a balanced diet.

o I think it is important to learn about good nutrition.
o I can prepare a healthy snack.
o I know what appropriate portion sizes look like for someone my size and weight.
o I think exercise is important.
o I like to eat fruits and vegetables.
o I eat too much junk food.
o I think advertising influences my food choices.

Methods to Maximize Engagement and Participation

- Some students may have a hard time forming an opinion immediately; these learners might be given some time in advance to prepare their responses, or you might choose to give all students time to construct a quick response to the prompts on paper, therefore giving everyone some practice in written expression and, specifically, in forming and defending an opinion.
- Post the numbers 1 through 5 in large print on chart paper and post these numbers along the wall so students see exactly where the markers are for each digit.
- To further help students clarify their position, you might ask them to add decimals to their response. Learners can then declare that they are a 1.5 as opposed to a 1.6 on a particular issue (might be an especially helpful addition for teachers of mathematics). To take the math practice a step further, you might even assign one or two students as *number crunchers*. Their job is to observe the line and average the score of the class on each point.

Another Version of This Activity ☼

This activity lends itself well to paired discussion. To form pairs or dyads in which students can exchange viewpoints on the topics, have the students line up based on their stand on any issue. Then break the line at the midpoint and literally double it back around so that the two students at each end are paired, and so on (e.g., 1 and 20 pair, 2 and 19 pair, 3 and 18 pair, etc.). Pairing students of opposing viewpoints allows them to stretch their perspectives.

Ideas for Using This Structure in My Classroom ✎

_____

_____

_____

_____

_____

_____

Creating Active Lectures 4

 ALL TOGETHER NOW!

When teachers want to elicit information from the group, they usually need to rely on asking one student at a time for an answer or for feedback. Although this strategy is sometimes quite appropriate, it can be limiting in that it keeps a few students actively engaged (and usually the same few students day after day) and sometimes leaves others to daydream or otherwise disconnect from class. To avoid this common pitfall, try some version of *All Together Now*, which involves asking for a response from all of your students at once.

Directions

- Ask a question or seek a response of some kind from the group.
- Let students know that you want them to respond in a new way. Tell them that instead of raising hands, you will be asking for another indication that they know the answer.
- This structure can take many forms, as students can be asked to respond using different methods and materials in different situations. Students can respond, for instance, using
  o mini-chalkboards or mini–wipe boards,
  o fingers or other parts of their bodies (e.g., hold up three fingers if you agree, two if you don't, and one if you are not sure; raise both of your arms if you feel strongly about what I said and only one if you do not),
  o movement and activity (e.g., walk to the front of the room if you can answer my question and to the back if you cannot), or
  o premade cards (e.g., students have cards naming the parts of speech and hold them up as the teacher writes words on the board; students have cards with different fractions written on them and hold them up as the teacher shows visual images of different pie graphs).

Examples

- A kindergarten teacher used *All Together Now* to introduce addition and subtraction to his students. He gave each student two laminated cards, one that represented addition (+) and one that represented subtraction (−). Using two frog puppets and some apples, he performed different scenes in which the frogs either lost apples or found them. After each scene, he asked students to indicate whether the scene involved addition or subtraction. Students, all at once, were required to hold up either their (+) card or their (−) card.

- A high school physics teacher gave students mini–wipe boards and asked a series of questions during his demonstration on momentum. He set up a ramp and rolled different-sized soup cans down it several times, each time making the ramp more or less steep. Using the boards, students were asked to make predictions throughout the demonstration (e.g., the can will roll faster or farther).

Methods to Maximize Engagement and Participation

- It may be particularly helpful in this structure to consciously engineer and monitor "think time" given to the students. A downfall of most large-group question-and-answer formats is that teachers ask for an answer in less than 10 seconds. Consequently, only the students who process verbal language quickly are able to respond. Try setting a timer, allowing at least 15 to 30 seconds for answer development. If you make this wait time routine, you can assign a student to be the time keeper who will call for a class response.
- Give students the opportunity to compare their individual ideas with a partner and then construct their response as a team. This process will decrease anxiety and increase greater individual confidence in the choral response.
- Assign one student who provides the correct answer verbally or on a card for the entire group. To challenge this student, provide a choice of two or more answers.
- Provide a "Tips Page" with keywords to prompt the recall of learned material. It can be available to all students but should be given to specific students who need extra support when questions are asked. This page can be reviewed before any questions are posed to the large group.
- Some students might be well suited to pose the questions to the large group or demonstrate the problem to be solved. As in the physics example previously, two students could make decisions and demonstrate the elements of momentum using the ramp and soup cans to quiz classmates.

Ideas for Using This Structure in My Classroom 🖊

_____

_____

_____

_____

_____

SHARE AND COMPARE

This strategy requires students to work both independently and interdependently. *Share and Compare* is a quick (one- to five-minute) support strategy that gives learners opportunities to check their note-taking abilities by collaborating with a peer. Instructors using this technique can help students take better notes and monitor whether they are able to identify the key ideas in the day's material.

It's important to remember that the purpose of this exercise is not to have students give their notes to one another, but instead to work cooperatively to fill gaps in their collective understanding of the information.

Directions

- This structure should be used in conjunction with a traditional lecture or whole-class discussion. Begin by asking students to take notes as they always would during such a lesson format.
- Then put learners into pairs (or have them work with the student sitting across from them) and direct them to share and compare notes, focusing on summarizing key information and locating misconceptions.
- Students can also generate questions or solve a problem posed by the instructor.

Example

A high school trigonometry teacher used *Share and Compare* as students took notes on applying the trigonometric formulas for finding the areas of triangles, circular sectors, and segments. Because the material was very new to all of the students and they were clearly struggling to understand it, he stopped the lecture every 10 minutes and asked pairs of students to share and compare notes. He asked them to pay particular attention to the accuracy of the information. As students worked together to improve their notes, he walked from dyad to dyad to answer questions and clarify concepts.

Methods to Maximize Engagement and Participation

- Not all learners need to start from a blank page when taking notes. Students with learning disabilities, cognitive disabilities, and some physical disabilities, as well as English Language Learners could be provided a set of guided notes to keep them on target during the lecture and to ensure that they will have accurate information to share.
- If some learners cannot participate using guided notes, the teacher can provide a completed set of notes for the lecture and require the student to participate in note taking by highlighting keywords or ideas and putting icons or other markings next to items they want to discuss with their peer partner.
- To make this exercise more challenging for certain students, identify students who typically take detailed, accurate, and complex notes and ask them to reteach a part of the lecture to the group.

Ideas for Using This Structure in My Classroom ✐

_____

_____

_____

_____

_____

_____

_____

_____

_____

_____

_____

_____

_____

_____

STAND AND DELIVER

This technique offers another alternative to the traditional question-and-answer format in which only a few students get to interact with the teacher. In contrast, *Stand and Deliver* allows every student to have his or her answer represented in a large-group discussion.

This structure promotes active listening because students must be attentive to others to determine if their responses are the same or different. It also promotes higher level thinking as students must make comparisons between their own answers and others. Benefits for the teacher in using this structure are that he or she can visually see which students hold the same answers and which are the most popular or prevalent answers.

Directions

- A question is posed, and each student formulates an answer. The question must be one that promotes a number of viable answers or solutions (e.g., "Suggest one way you could help stop harassment in this school").
- After students have time to generate an answer, all class members stand.
- Call on one student at a time to share his or her answer aloud.
- When an answer is given by one student, everyone who shares the same answer should sit down (including the person called on). Another person is called on, and those who are still standing must determine if their answer is the same or similar enough to take a seat.
- Repeat the process until no one is left standing.

Example

During a seventh-grade unit about sexism in fairy tales, students were asked to think of a story they had been told or had read that represented women as evil characters. Students were paired up and given time to discuss their ideas. Cayden, a student who is nonverbal and has cognitive disabilities, was provided actual books to examine to convey his answer to his peer. The peer recorded Cayden's answer on his augmentative communication system so that he could share when called on. This exercise gave the teacher a measure of what fairy tales were familiar to her class. After listing the class answers, the teacher asked students to further analyze the types of evil women who were represented (e.g., stepmothers, sisters, old women, women who have magical powers).

Methods to Maximize Engagement and Participation

- Students can be put into groups and be given time to discuss answers or opinions; when they stand, each person must represent a different viewpoint (not his or her own) that was discussed.
- A student who may not be able to make a reliable assessment about whether his or her own answer is sufficiently different from the others

might be called on first so an assessment of other classmate responses is unnecessary. This suggestion may also be helpful for students who might sit down immediately to avoid participation. If called on first, they will be required to share an answer verbally.

- Students can work in pairs or small groups to produce a single answer and can sit down together, which speeds up the timeframe needed for this activity and gives students opportunities to learn how to collaborate and synthesize ideas.

- When individual accountability is a concern, students can be asked to write a brief statement or jot notes about their answers so that the teacher can check that a response was formulated.

Ideas for Using This Structure in My Classroom

_____

_____

_____

_____

_____

_____

_____

_____

_____

_____

_____

_____

_____

CHANTS AND RANTS

To begin a lesson, to reinforce a concept, or simply to get students more involved in whole-class learning, try the effective and amusing *Chants and Rants.* Asking students to repeat key phrases, words, or ideas certainly gets students more alert and engaged, but using chants or other types of choral response has the additional benefit of improving learners' chances of remembering the material long after the lesson is over.

Directions

- When designing a lecture, choose words, core concepts, ideas, or a phrase that you want students to remember.
- Then, develop a catchy or memorable way to repeat, sing, or chant this information.
- Next, identify potential points in the lecture to interject the chant. A routine chant might be used at the beginning of a class session to reinforce behavioral expectations or raise the energy level. Other chants can be used in the context of the lecture to reinforce content and cue students that the information is critical.
- Chants are most effective when they can be used repeatedly over time. Concepts that occur in several contexts or are foundations for other skills are good choices for chants.

Implementation Tip ✋

Although teachers may be most familiar with chants that rhyme (e.g., "Thirty days hath September, April, June, and November . . ."), content doesn't need to be poetic or done in singsong fashion to be memorable. Just asking students to verbally repeat important information (and use gestures or physical movements if appropriate) can be a powerful learning strategy. *Chants and Rants* can be used daily and without much or any planning.

Examples

- A high school physics teacher told us that he often asked his students to chant, "Fission *and* fusion release energy" during lectures on the topic. He shared that it was not uncommon for former students to approach him on the street (years after they had taken his class) and shout, "Fission *and* fusion release energy."
- A teacher in a fifth-grade classroom used this regular chant to set behavioral expectations before the start of some lessons or when classroom management needed to be checked. To the tune of "Respect" (sung by Aretha Franklin) he would chant the lead vocal, changing a few key words, with the students responding as backup singers:

Teacher:	R-E-S-P-E-C-T . . . that's what YOU need for ME!
Teacher:	R-E-S-P-E-C-T. Find out what it means to me.
Teacher:	Oh!
Students:	Sock it to me, sock it to me, sock it to me, sock it to me
Teacher:	A little respect
Students:	Sock it to me, sock it to me, sock it to me, sock it to me
Teacher:	Whoa, babe
Students:	Just a little bit
Teacher:	A little respect
Students:	Just a little bit
Teacher:	I get tired
Students:	Just a little bit
Teacher:	Keep on tryin'
Students:	Just a little bit
Teacher:	You're runnin' out of foolin'
Students:	Just a little bit
Teacher:	And I ain't lyin'
Students:	Just a little bit
All together:	(re, re, re, re) 'spect

In most instances, this was enough to set the tone or alter the classroom climate. Sometimes the teacher would follow the chant with a quick request from the students to shout out what respect should look like and sound like in their classroom.

- A middle-school English teacher wrote the following rap (to the tune of *Yankee Doodle*) for his students during a unit on the Harlem Renaissance:

Langston Hughes was a poet

Wrote novels and stories too

Part of the Harlem Renaissance

His fame just grew and grew.

Students chanted the poem during parts of the teacher's lecture on famous figures of the movement. At the end of the lecture, students were asked to construct their own rap or song on any individual considered part of the Harlem Renaissance.

- During a lecture on geometry vocabulary, two coteaching partners (a general education math teacher and a special education teacher) asked their students to do a call-and-response exercise with the following text. Initially, the teachers modeled the chant with one taking the role of the students and one taking the role of the teachers. Then, they asked students to join in:

Teacher and students:	Talking about angles!
Teachers:	Angles.

Students:	Angles.
Teachers and students:	Please define . . .
Teachers:	An angle is formed . . .
Students:	An angle is formed . . .
Teachers:	When two rays have the same endpoint.
Students:	When two rays have the same endpoint.
Teachers:	How many rays?
Students:	Two rays.
Teachers:	What is the endpoint called, I ask?
Students:	Vertex.
Teachers and students:	The common endpoint is the vertex.
Teachers:	Vertex?
Students:	Vertex!
Teachers:	One ray forms the initial side.
Students:	The initial side.
Teachers:	One ray is the terminal side.
Students:	The terminal side.
Teachers and students:	Talking about angles!

Students were invited to stand and move around during the exercise and eventually to write their own verses related to angles. Several students with learning disabilities in this class found that this technique helped them to stay attentive during the instructor's long lectures and retain the information he was teaching. To differentiate the materials, the special and general education math teachers wrote down the words and audiotaped the class during the chant so students could study the concepts auditorially and visually.

Methods to Maximize Engagement and Participation

- Write the words on the chant down on the board or on an overhead so students can follow along.
- Give students who may need extra assistance a copy of the words with their part of the chant highlighted in a bright color.
- When appropriate, pair the chant with movements or motions. For instance, if you are using chanting to help students learn Spanish verbs, they can both say the words and act them out.
- Allow students to participate in crafting the chants when possible; you might give them a familiar rhyme or melody to use as a starting point.
- Audiotape the chants or videotape the class engaged in the act so you can play tapes back for students at points during lectures or right before test time. A student who is nonverbal or has significant physical disabilities

may be given the job of recording the class as they chant. Recording can be accomplished with a small tape player activated by a single pressure switch (like the one featured in the *Carousel* example). Once recorded, the chant can be initiated by the student for the whole class to follow using this same technology to start and stop the tape.

- Young children are typically quite willing to join in on chanting exercises. It is common, for instance, for a teacher to ask elementary-aged students to chant certain number patterns in unison; this is how many of us learned to count by 2s or by 10s. Older students may be more reluctant to participate, but their interest may be piqued if the strategy is introduced as a rap rather than as a chant or rhyme.

Ideas for Using This Structure in My Classroom

_____

_____

_____

_____

_____

_____

_____

_____

_____

_____

_____

_____

_____

_____

THE WHIP

The purpose of this activity is to increase the number of students who speak up in whole-class discussions, to give students practice in self-management, and to give communication practice to those who need it. For these reasons, *The Whip* (Harmin, 1994; Harmin & Toth, 2006) may be an especially attractive structure for teachers who have many students with communication-related disabilities or those who are learning English as a second language.

This structure can be used with all or part of the class. In other words, the teacher can "whip around" the entire classroom, or he or she can choose to get a sampling of student ideas by using this structure down one row of the classroom or with just one small group.

Directions

- Put forth a topic or question. Students are then quickly expected to generate some type of response to it. Several different types of prompts can be used for this activity, including the following:
  ○ sentence starters (I think good grammar is important because _____. An ethical scientist always _____.),
  ○ open-ended questions (How do you think Hitler was able to get Germans to cooperate with his plan? What is one good way to prepare for a test?), and
  ○ fact-based questions (What is one state capital? What is 100 divisible by? What is one healthy food? What is one action word?)
- After giving everyone a few moments to think of an answer, point to an individual student (usually one sitting in the front or back of a row) and ask for a response.
- After getting a response from the first student, continue down the row and one by one, ask each student to share an answer.
- Encourage students who cannot think of an answer or those who get frustrated when their answer is used by a classmate to repeat another student's answer.

Examples

- A second-grade teacher ended a lesson on the characteristics of living things with *The Whip*. She "whipped" around the entire room, asking each student to name one living thing.
- A third-grade teacher started a lesson on estimation by asking all students to name a time when they estimated something.
- A high school physical education teacher used *The Whip* to review a unit on football. He did a quick whip with a handful of students, asking them to complete the sentence, "One rule of football we learned is _____."
- A middle-school choral music teacher had all of her students watch a videotape of the group's last performance and asked everyone to answer the question, "How did we do?" in no more than six words.

Implementation Tip ✋

If you want to use this structure when you are short on time, consider giving students some parameters to keep in mind when constructing their responses. For instance, you can tell them that they each have 15 seconds or only seven words to express an idea or give their answer.

Methods to Maximize Engagement and Participation

- Let some or all students use flashcards or mini-chalkboards to share a written response.
- Preteach the content to learners who need it; give suggestions for content they might share.
- Give students the option of passing when their turn comes.
- Remind all students that repeating an answer is not only okay, it may also be helpful to the group because students are likely to remember content, ideas, and concepts that they hear several times.
- Select students to be first in the whip who may have difficulty assessing if an answer has been given or may have a limited repertoire of answers.
- Whip around the classroom several times so students needing repeated practice in sharing ideas aloud can get it and so all learners can hear important information shared from different perspectives and voices.

Ideas for Using This Structure in My Classroom ✐

NUMBERED HEADS TOGETHER

Some teachers find that even when they give students time to share ideas in small groups, the same students dominate the discussion as they did in the large group. *Numbered Heads Together*, a structure developed and popularized by Spencer Kagan (1992), is one way to encourage participation by all, help the instructor solicit responses from a greater range of students, and give everyone an equal chance to be the expert.

Directions

- Arrange students in teams of three or four, and assign each individual a number (e.g., Pete is 1, Yolanda is 2, Amir is 3, Allison is 4).
- Assign the groups a question to answer, an idea to brainstorm, or a task to complete. For example, you might ask students to name everything they know about ancient Rome or to generate a list of conductors and semiconductors.
- Encourage everyone to participate and contribute. Then, give the groups a set time to answer the question and to make sure that everyone in their group can answer the question. Explicitly explain that all students are responsible for the learning of all others. Therefore, Pete is not only responsible for providing an answer to the question, but he also needs to make sure that Amir, Yolanda, and Allison can answer the question.
- After giving teams some time to work, ask the question again and call out a student number (e.g., "Tell me what you already know about ancient Rome. I want to hear answers from all 4s").
- The student with that particular number should stand; he or she is responsible for reporting to peers and the teacher.
- You can then ask each of these students to report to the large group.

Implementation Tip ✋

Consider forming Numbered Heads groups early in the school year and keeping students in these groups year round. This way, you can quickly move into the structure during a lecture or discussion without having students count off or get acquainted with those in the group. When students enter the classroom on a given day, you can inform them they will be using Numbered Heads Together and can choose or structure their desks accordingly. This ongoing use of the structure might be especially powerful in inclusive classrooms, as you will want to help students immediately understand that they will be regularly supporting and teaching each other and working collaboratively.

Example

A middle-school teacher of a general music class put students into *Numbered Heads Together* formation for the last 15 minutes of the day every Friday. The groups remained the same all year (so students never forgot where they needed to be) but the questions changed weekly. Sometimes, the teacher would ask students questions about curriculum, such as, "What are some characteristics of classical music?" Other times, the questions were aimed at helping students know one another better and work together more effectively. For instance, at the beginning of the year, the teacher asked students to discuss, "How can our group work together effectively?"

Methods to Maximize Engagement and Participation

- Call on two students to answer together ("I want 2s and 4s to collaboratively give a response").
- If a particular student would have a difficult time sharing in a large group format, have students write a collective response or responses on paper and give it to that student to hold up or hand to the teacher.
- If a class member is nonverbal, the teacher can allow sufficient time for the group to record the answer on the student's augmentative communication system, like the LightWRITER (shown in Figure 4.1), a portable, text-to-speech communication aid for individuals with speech impairments. When a number is called, any student in the group, including the learner who is nonverbal, can use this portable keyboard with speech output to respond to the question.

Figure 4.1   LightWRITER

- If some students are dominating discussions in this format, provide additional rules, such as "Everyone must speak once before anyone speaks twice." To make this part of the process more concrete, some teachers use sticks, pebbles, or other markers. Each student receives one or two markers, for instance, and must contribute one to a common pile each time he or she makes a remark. When a student's markers are gone, he must wait until everyone else dispenses of their markers to contribute again to the discussion.

Ideas for Using This Structure in My Classroom ✎

_____

_____

_____

_____

_____

_____

_____

_____

_____

_____

_____

_____

TAKE MY PERSPECTIVE, PLEASE!

This interactive exercise promotes a number of important skills that include developing a position statement or response to a question, using attentive listening, paraphrasing, having individual accountability, and perspective taking. *Take My Perspective, Please!* prompts 100% participation of a class and can be used at the beginning of a session to generate interest in the subject matter, in the middle to check for understanding, or at the end to reinforce key learning points.

Directions

- To engage in this activity, provide a note card to every student and direct students to write their names anywhere on the card.
- Then provide a question or response prompt that relates to the subject or topic of concern. The best prompts for this activity should be those that have multiple correct answers or encourage diverse positions. For example,
  - Should all public smoking be banned?
  - Consider the rule of the first female pharaoh. Why do you think we have not had a female president in the history of the United States?
  - We've learned about successful experiments with animal cloning. What is your position on human cloning?
- Allow students time to formulate an answer to the prompt. Encourage them to jot notes to themselves on the card that will help them remember their key points, but tell them that full sentences do not need to be used.
- Cue the students to stand up, move to a new location in the room, and find a partner. With note card in hand, partners should exchange ideas verbally. Alert students that they should listen attentively to their partner and paraphrase what has been said, because they will need to represent their partner's ideas.
- After sufficient time is given to swap ideas, tell students to exchange note cards and "take the perspective" of their partner. After this exchange, cue students to find another partner and repeat the interchange. However, this time they must assume the identity of their previous partner and represent their perspective. Have them repeat the process several times.
- You can decide how many partner exchanges are feasible given the instructional timeframe.
- On returning to a large-group arrangement, ask specific students to share the perspective they have assumed. This can also be a time to check with the originator of the perspective to determine if the information was passed along accurately.

Implementation Tip 🖐

Younger students will find it more challenging to retain detailed information across repeated exchanges. When first teaching this structure, it may be necessary to start with an exchange of simple information (e.g., my favorite TV show is . . .) and reduce the rounds of exchanges to one or two.

Example

A math teacher used *Take My Perspective, Please!* to encourage students to consider diverse approaches to solutions. Students were provided a graph representing linear equations related to the increase or decrease of male and female doctors over a 40-year period (1960–2000). Questions drawn from the school's math curriculum materials that were posed at different points in activity included the following:

- o How would you describe the trends shown in the data points and the linear models that have been drawn to match patterns in those points?
- o Why do you suppose the percentage of women doctors has been increasing over the past 40 years?
- o Would you expect the trend in the graph to continue 10 or 20 years into the future? This means 10 or 20 years beyond 2000.
- o How would you go about finding equations for linear models of the data trends?
- o If you were asked to make a report on future prospects for numbers of male and female doctors, what kinds of questions could you answer using the linear models? (Core-Plus Mathematics Project, 2005)

Students were given some time to study the graphs and formulate their own ideas for responses before engaging in the idea exchange. Afterward, the mathematics teacher asked the students to analyze and, if appropriate, graph the patterns in responses they had heard.

Methods to Maximize Engagement and Participation

- Let students generate the relevant question to ask based on a reading or short introduction of the subject by the teacher. Midway through the session, the question could be changed or expanded.
- This structure poses similar issues noted in other descriptions regarding the spontaneous development of a position or statement. Some students with language, communication, or processing difficulties may find it problematic; therefore, provide adequate latency or preview time to develop a response.
- The note card with a classmate's ideas on it serves as a built-in "cheat sheet" for partners to remember the new perspective. However, this still may be too challenging for particular students. Therefore, some students may be allowed to keep their own position throughout the session. The repetition of the same statement may help build confidence and promote personal elaboration on the topic.
- A useful piece of assistive technology for students who are nonverbal or simply need a reminder of the concepts they need to share would be the Step-by-Step voice output device (see Figure 4.2). This device could be used to record a student's position and then be rerecorded each time he or she encounters a new student. There are 75 seconds of recording time. Each touch of the switch plays and advances messages in sequence. There is also a message-repeat feature to replay one message in the series.

Figure 4.2   Step-by-Step Communicator

Source: Image courtesy of AbleNet, Inc.

Ideas for Using This Structure in My Classroom ✏

_____

_____

_____

_____

_____

_____

_____

_____

_____

_____

_____

_____

_____

_____

_____

_____

_____

_____

LECTURE REFLECTIONS

Using this structure, teachers build regular stopping points into their lectures for students to reflect on and react to the information that has been delivered. Responding to a number of sentence starters can help students relate the content immediately to their current knowledge base and provide a quick check of understanding for the teacher. The nature of student responses can provide direction to the teacher to reteach content, move forward in the curriculum, or make clarifications.

Directions

- During the preparation of a lecture that ranges anywhere from 10 minutes to one hour, identify several logical stopping points suitable to reflection. A general rule to follow is to intersperse reflection points every 10 to 15 minutes.
- Before the lecture begins, tell the students that there will be several breaks or stopping points in the lecture to reflect and write a short response.
- At the planned stopping points, provide a sentence starter and allow sufficient time for students to write a brief response, then begin the lecture again.
- Students can continue to write additional reflections on the same paper. At subsequent stopping points, it may be useful to ask several students to share their reflections aloud.
- After the lecture, collect and review the responses. Student work may reveal misunderstandings or needs that provide direction for instruction in the next day's session.
- A number of potential sentence starters for reflections are
  - I think . . .
  - I wonder . . .
  - What's hard about this is . . .
  - What puzzles me is . . .
  - I am unsure about . . .
  - What's interesting is . . .
  - One area that I need further practice is . . .
  - A strength for me is . . .
  - Something I need to work harder on is . . .
  - It was great when . . .
  - I was surprised that . . .
  - I already knew about . . . but learned that . . .
  - Others say this about (the topic) . . .
  - I learned . . .
  - It's okay that . . .
  - I am concerned that . . .
  - I am affirmed when . . .
  - I feel secure when . . .

○ I think what will happen is . . .
○ This is different because . . .
○ I feel confident about . . .
○ It made me think of . . .
○ I could visualize . . .
○ I figured out . . .

Implementation Tip ✋

It's very helpful to share the purpose for using this active lecture technique with your students, as some may be puzzled about the change in the pace and rhythm of the classroom. Letting them in on the rationale for this type of instruction can give them insight into their own learning and may, consequently, give them motivation to participate and give them an idea to use when they are in charge of teaching their peers (e.g., science fair, class presentations).

Example

During an introductory science lecture for sixth graders on the topic of plate tectonics and the earth's structure, the instructor interjected the following set of reflections for the purpose of checking for student understanding and background knowledge:

○ A concept that kind of confused me was . . .
○ I already knew about . . . but learned . . .
○ Tomorrow, I'd like you to review . . .
○ I could visualize . . .

In this bilingual classroom there were a number of English Language Learners, so at each table, the instructor had the sentence starters on a sheet of paper in English and in Spanish as well as a set of science vocabulary from the lecture in both languages from which any student could select to help construct a response. Sample vocabulary or phrases that could be used to complete the sentence starters included layers of the Earth, location of plate boundaries, types of plate motion, continental drift, seafloor spreading, and Pangea.

Methods to Maximize Engagement and Participation

- Combine *Lecture Reflections* with other types of breaks or active lecture techniques (*Chants and Rants*) to keep the process fresh and interesting, but follow the rule not to talk continuously for any more than 10 to 20 minutes, that is, about 10 to 15 minutes for elementary or middle-school students and about 15 to 20 minutes for high school learners.
- Instead of providing just one option as a sentence starter, provide a short list of three or four from which students can choose.
- For students who are unable to write well spontaneously or who may have difficultly formulating a complete response in the time offered,

prepare a number of pretyped responses that can be read and selected as a response (as in the previous example).

- Periodically, allow students to turn and talk to one another after the sentence starter is given, and ask for responses verbally rather than in writing.
- Place charts around the room with various sentence starters that are appropriate for any stopping point in the lecture. Have students get up and write responses on a chart of their choice at each lecture break.
- Create multiple-choice response cards that include keywords or pictures that can be circled to indicate a response (see Figure 4.3).

Figure 4.3   Response Cards

This is how I feel about the material so far . . .

I feel good and understand it.   *I'm confused.*

Ideas for Using This Structure in My Classroom ✐

STOP THE LECTURE AND START THE DRAMA

To bring out the drama kings and queens in the classroom, assign students to engage in a short role play or skit at specific points in the class session to demonstrate their understanding of classroom material. These quickly planned sketches can be a serious rendition of important facts or can be developed as parodies and satires of a situation. These role plays work best to illustrate key events, demonstrate roles of critical figures in history, or show the process of a tangible sequence. Props are optional!

Directions

- Just as noted in the previous structure for *Lecture Reflections,* the instructor should identify in advance specific stopping points in the lecture, at which time a role play can be demonstrated. The teacher may choose several different points to allow groups to take turns being on stage.
- Before the lecture begins, tell the students that they will be responsible for creating a skit or scenario that represents some aspect of the lecture content. The instructor may want to identify the scenarios in advance so the students can be alert to salient points and details in the instructor's lecture. To facilitate a smooth transition to the activity, identify the size and members of the role-play groups before beginning the lecture.
- At the planned stopping points, the teacher provides the topic of the scenario to be represented. Some examples might be to replay great moments in history such as the discovery of electricity, Rosa Parks being arrested for refusing to ride in the back of the bus, Japanese families arriving at an internment camp, or primitive man learning to use fire.
- Twists of humor that force critical comparisons can be fostered by blending current and past viewpoints. For example, ask teams to role play an air traffic controller commenting on the first flight of the Wright brothers, make Attila the Hun appear in Judge Judy's court, or place the leaders of two warring countries on the *Dr. Phil* show.
- After the role plays, the student audience and teacher make comments and relevant teaching points.

Example

After presenting a comparison of women's rights across key eras of history, a tenth-grade world history teacher posed the following scenario: "Imagine Nefertiti, Sojourner Truth, Eleanor Roosevelt, Betty Friedan, and Hillary Clinton getting together for lunch and comparing their rights as women." To facilitate participation of a student with learning disabilities and ensure that all students came to the role play with information to share, the instructor provided a guide for strategic note taking (Boyle, 2001) as shown in Figure 4.4.

Figure 4.4   Strategic Note-Taking Form for Women's Rights Lecture

Fill in this portion before the lecture begins. ✎

What is today's topic?

Describe what you know about the topic:

As the instructor lectures, take the following notes. ✎

Name three to seven main points with details about today's topic as they are being discussed.

* _____

* _____

* _____

* _____

* _____

* _____

* _____

Summary—Briefly describe how the ideas or information on women's rights across historical eras are similar or related:

Summary—Briefly describe how the ideas or information on women's rights across historical eras are different:

New Vocabulary or Terms:

* _____   * _____

* _____   * _____

* _____   * _____

Methods to Maximize Engagement and Participation

- To get students comfortable with the look and feel of the skits, give a demonstration. If you coteach with partners (e.g., therapist, general or special educator, principal), get together and show students how it's done! If you don't have partners in the classroom, this activity might be a nice time to start a collaboration. If you want your speech therapist, social worker, or English as a Second Language teacher to work in your general education classroom on a more regular basis, introduce them to the class in this fun and entertaining way.

- For students who are not yet ready to be the primary actors in the role play, ensure that they have contributed ideas to the skit and are in charge of some aspect of the presentation (e.g., be in charge of props or have a nonspeaking role).

- Rather than having one group perform in front of the whole class, arrange small group-to-group demonstrations, which can be less intimidating. This format also expedites the process, and students have more time to perform their skits.

- Some students might be assigned roles as skit judges (á la *American Idol*) and be encouraged to score performances and offer pithy comments.

- For a student with disabilities who may have trouble changing roles frequently or acting out ever-changing information, consider the use of role plays that have a consistent character, common introduction, or guided narration. This can promote the student becoming expert and comfortable with a dependable role.

Ideas for Using This Structure in My Classroom

_____

_____

_____

_____

_____

_____

_____

_____

_____

_____

_____

_____

ROUNDTABLE

Roundtable (Kagan, 1992) is a collaborative technique that begins with a blank sheet of paper and ends with the creation of a common product that can be a list, a paragraph, or even a picture. Originally designed as a general brainstorming technique, it also can be used for review, as a check for understanding during a lecture, or to focus attention during a movie or video.

Directions

- Seat groups around a table with one pencil and one piece of paper. Then pose a question and have students take turns recording answers on the paper as it is passed around the table.
- The question should be carefully chosen. It should have multiple answers, and all students should be capable of answering it in some way (e.g., What roles did women play during World War II? What strategies do you use for multiplying?). When time is called, teams count their responses written on the paper. Answers are then shared by the entire class.
- If appropriate, the teacher can ask groups to read and evaluate their lists for the most creative or "on target" responses or ask groups to summarize lists in a few sentences.

Examples

- A second-grade teacher asked students to answer the question, "What makes our community unique?" First, students discussed the question with their group members. Then, they silently passed a sheet around the group, and every child added one or two words related to their discussion.
- As sixth-grade students were watching a documentary on endangered species, the teacher gave one sheet to small roundtable groups of six. When the film started, the first student watched until he or she could find a response to the question, "What is one thing you learned about endangered species?" Then he or she jotted a response on the sheet and passed it to the next student. When that student was able to answer the question, he or she jotted a response and continued to pass the sheet. When the sixth student in the group added an answer to the question, he or she passed it back to the first student to begin the process anew. Students took turns in this way until the film ended.
- During a mini-lecture by the tenth-grade family and consumer educator about child development, each table of students was given a sheet of paper to collectively write a set of notes. As the instructor proceeded with content, the first person wrote down an important point then passed on the paper. The notes pages were reviewed with the teacher for accuracy and then duplicated for the class. A student with Asperger's syndrome in this class was not always able to select the most salient information from the teacher's lecture during his turn. To support his participation, the teacher watched for his acquisition of the *Roundtable* paper and emphasized an

opportunity for note taking. For example, she would pause and say, "This is an important point" and then write it on the board as a cue for the student.

- In a high school art class, the instructor transformed an individual assignment into a collective project by using *Roundtable*. A sculpture project to create clay masks had been a typical assignment carried out alone by each class member. To use the *Roundtable* technique, the teacher placed students in groups of four or five and provided one lump of clay to the first student in the team. That student made one contribution to the ball of clay to begin making a mask (e.g., shaping a nose), then handed it to the next student, who added a second feature before passing it on. The clay "changed hands" throughout the class session with each person adding a new feature or changing the element that previous teammates had created. This collective method worked well for a student in class with a severe physical disability who could add an undefined feature (e.g., a small lump of clay added for an ear) that would then be refined or embellished by the next person to receive the mask.

Methods to Maximize Engagement and Participation

- Allow a student who cannot write or talk to point to an existing response with which he or she agrees. A tally mark can then be placed by that response.
- Give students stickers containing two or three responses; when they get the page, they attach one of the stickers to the roundtable paper.
- Give students the option of adding graphics, highlighting a favorite response, or writing a phrase on the paper.

Another Version of This Activity ✿

Give all students in the group a piece of paper with a different question at the top. When the teacher says "begin," students write one response to the question on the paper. When the teacher says "switch," each student passes his or her paper to the right and adds an answer to the question on that page. The process continues until all students have responded to every question at the table.

Ideas for Using This Structure in My Classroom ✎

_____

_____

_____

_____

_____

Assessing and Celebrating 5

ARE YOU GAME?

Most teachers realize that games are motivating and fun for students of any age. They may not understand, however, how much learners can profit from playing and, in this case, creating their own games. Students will surely be excited to engage in this structure and may even surprise the teacher by using their creations outside of the classroom and extending their learning beyond the confines of a particular unit.

Directions

- Put learners into pairs or small groups, and ask them to create a board game that will teach the players about the curriculum being studied. Students might be given anywhere from 15 minutes to several hours to construct their game.
- Provide a range of materials to each group, including paper, poster board, markers, dice, spinners and markers (from other board games in the classroom), and index cards.
- Introduce any rules up front. For example,
  - "The game must have a name related to our course content" (e.g., "Prime Number Pop Quiz" or "Fun With Figurative Language");
  - "The game must help us learn about _____" (e.g., nouns, integers, the future, living things); and
  - "The game must have simple rules that students in this classroom can easily read and follow."

Implementation Tip 🖐

If time is at a premium, have students construct card games instead of board games.

Example

Students in one sixth-grade class were responsible for creating board games after studying China for several weeks. They were to select one piece of the unit to use as the area of focus for the game (e.g., geography, recent history). One team created a game based on China's geography; they called it "China: Surrounded by the Seas." Players had to "travel" from Mongolia to the Yellow Sea, the East China Sea, or the South China Sea answering questions about the 14 border countries of China and the various provinces of the nation as they moved from square to square. The teacher strategically assigned different roles to different students in the groups. One student, Suj, who has a cognitive disability, was working on an individual goal of "locating China on a map." His role was to draw and label a map of Asia on the game board and on the cover of the game box while other students took on the responsibilities of researching questions and designing the board.

Methods to Maximize Engagement and Participation

- Assign students different roles in their groups to make sure that each learner participates in a meaningful way (e.g., art director, information gatherer).
- Provide sufficient examples of different types of games, and allow students to review the rules and materials of some of the games that are kept in the classroom.
- If some of your students want an additional challenge, you might allow them to design a computer game; students may need additional instruction in programming from a technology teacher for this task.
- If some students are struggling to create an original idea (or if time is limited), let them use an existing game board and materials and have them adapt the rules and questions instead.
- You can challenge all or some students by asking them to create a game that could possibly be produced for a larger group. Older students, in particular, might be able to create a unique product that could be used across classrooms in the district or even in the local area. Some students may even want to engage in market research or work with a local toy store to further develop their ideas.

Ideas for Using This Structure in My Classroom ✎

_____

_____

_____

_____

_____

_____

DESKTOP TEACHING

Desktop Teaching is an active learning strategy designed to give students the opportunity to act as both teachers and learners (Draper, 1997; Parker, 1990). Students teach one another in a fair-like atmosphere; each prepares a lesson lasting from 5 to 10 minutes based on a topic or objective that is assigned to them or that they have chosen. Although this format works very well for formal presentations such as those commonly associated with science fairs or final assessments, *Desktop Teaching* can also be used more informally to review or reinforce content after just a day or two.

Directions

- Provide time for students to develop a short teaching sequence related to the subject at hand.
- After students have their information prepared, have about half of the students set up materials on their desks for teaching, while the remaining students move from "teacher" to "teacher," participating in the lessons.
- The students who are teaching rotate with the students who are learning so as to have the opportunity to participate in the lessons prepared by their peers. The students continue moving around the room until each member of the class has attended the lessons prepared by all of his or her classmates.
- Encourage students to include visual aids and other learning materials, demonstrations, and short audience-participation activities in their lessons.

Implementation Tip ✋

Take some time to teach the students about good teaching; give them tips for staying within time limits, presenting information in a memorable way, and eliciting participation from their audience. You might even share some of the strategies in this book with your students. If possible, give students time to rehearse their lesson with a partner.

Examples

- Students in a seventh-grade industrial technology class used *Desktop Teaching* as a way to showcase their learning at the end of the year. Each student in the class chose an independent study topic to explore in depth. As part of their desktop display, students were required to have at least one model or visual representation for their presentation and a short handout that their classmates could study and keep. Some of the desktop lessons developed were tension and compression forces, bridge design, ancient technologies, and computer programming. This hands-on structure, although beneficial for every active learner in the classroom, was very helpful for the eight students in the classroom who used English as a second language, as these learners were able to both hear and see the concepts being studied. Furthermore, they were able to practice conversational English while engaged in academic work.

- During a social studies unit featuring great peacemakers of the world, a fifth-grade teacher asked students to use the Internet to gather information about individuals who had been or currently are peacemakers (e.g., Gandhi and Wangari Maathi, the Kenyan environmentalist). Each student was expected to use the information to prepare a short report for *Desktop Teaching.* James, a student with language-learning disabilities, found it difficult to stay on topic as well as share the most salient points of a report without providing excessive and sometimes unrelated details. To help keep his desktop presentation succinct and relevant, he was assisted by his teacher to construct a picture-based semantic web with Kidspiration Software as he gathered information from the Internet. This program helps create visual diagrams and written outlines. James constructed a visual diagram to organize the main and supporting topics of his verbal report about Mahatma Gandhi. The graphic assisted him to organize his thinking about the primary topics before the

Figure 5.1   Graphic Organizer of Gandhi Using Kidspiration

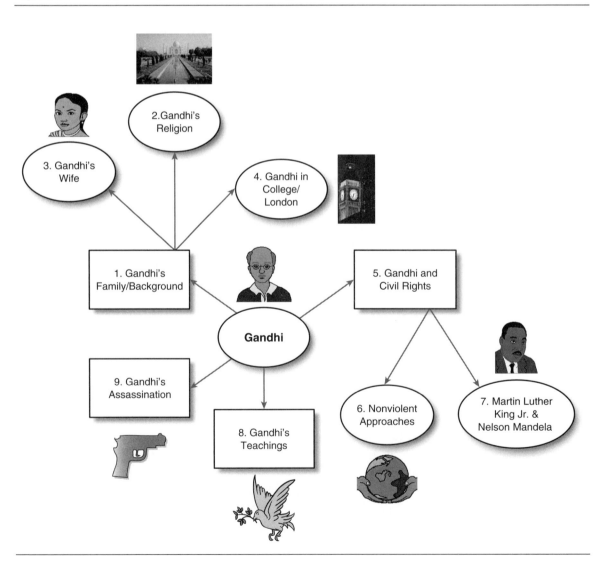

presentation and self-monitor the amount of detail he intended to share with his classmates. See Figure 5.1 for an example of the semantic map.

Methods to Maximize Engagement and Participation

- If a student has a special interest, he or she may be encouraged to incorporate it into the presentation. For example, a student who enjoys sports may want to include a game of some sort in his or her lesson.
- Encourage students to teach using their strengths; if a student loves to draw, encourage him or her to use visuals to convey information. If a student is a "techie," allow him or her to present using PowerPoint.
- Give timid students time and space to rehearse their presentations. For those who continue to struggle with public speaking, consider videotaping their rehearsals and playing the video during the desktop exchange. The student would still need to be available for questions and the reactions of his or her classmates.
- Presentations can also be videotaped at the time of the desktop event and be available to students, who can benefit from hearing the information repeated.
- Encourage learners to develop a theme for their lesson to increase student motivation and make the presentation itself memorable for all students. For example, a student in one classroom taught her classmates about the coordinate grid and graphing lines using an "under the sea" theme. She made a large, blue coordinate grid to represent the sea, and she had students plot points to represent the fish and lines to represent the seaweed (Draper, 1997).

Ideas for Using This Structure in My Classroom ✐

_____

_____

_____

_____

_____

_____

_____

_____

_____

_____

_____

GALLERY WALK

This structure can make an ordinary day in the classroom seem more refined and sophisticated! *Gallery Walk* allows students to play the part of museum visitor and artist and gives them a chance to represent their thoughts visually instead of in words. This structure is an easy and efficient way to summarize learning from a day, month, or year, and it engenders a sense of togetherness and cooperation as each image is a product of "group think."

Directions

- Students will work in groups of three to five for this activity.
- To begin, provide an idea that can be represented visually. This does not mean, however, that the idea has to be concrete. Sometimes abstract concepts inspire the most interesting visual products.
- Then, decide on what type of product you want students to produce. You might choose, for instance, an outline, a collage, a map, or a graphic organizer. For instance, a teacher might ask students to "illustrate a street scene from New York City in 1900," "paint a scene from the Native American legend, *The Buffalo and the Mouse*," "draw the water cycle," or "create a Venn diagram comparing and contrasting geometry and algebra."
- Give the group a set amount of time, and then ask students to display their work on a designated wall in the classroom.
- Have one student from the group stay by the poster and serve as the spokesperson; the job of this person is to present the product to those who "visit." Direct the other students to roam around the room, examine the posters, talk to the spokesperson from each group, and discuss the gallery products with each other.

Examples

- Students in an eighth-grade science class learned about simple machines, and then the teacher assigned one type of machine to each group. Students had to create a poster of their machine, including a few drawings and some examples showing how their machine is used in daily life. Students had a class period to create their poster and another period to engage in the gallery walk. During the walk, students brought clipboards and were instructed to take notes on new things they learned. This activity served as a unit review. To challenge those who had a more sophisticated understanding of the concepts, the teacher invited local engineers (mostly parents of students in the school) to visit the gallery and exchange ideas with the students.
- In a high school family and consumer education class, the teacher used this structure to teach the concept of "responsibility." She asked students, in groups of three, to think about the word *responsibility* (as it related to family, personal growth, and adult life) and discuss the ideas they connected to this word. Then the teacher had each group create a

piece of art representing the word. They were given only 20 minutes to create the art (which inspired creativity). They were also given limited materials to use but were allowed to use anything from their lockers, purses, or pockets (which inspired great variety in the responses). Then all of the students had an opportunity to travel around the room, examine the creations, and share any observations by speaking into a tape recorder that was available near each product. This activity was used as a beginning-of-the-year introduction to all of the year's topics, including work and vocational choices, pregnancy and family planning, personal finance, and independent living.

Methods to Maximize Engagement and Participation

- Depending on the needs and abilities of students, ask class members to take on other specific roles during the observation piece of the activity. A student may serve as a reporter, for instance, and be responsible for interviewing the "gallery patrons," or a student may be asked to serve as the gallery photographer so the visual information is captured for future study.
- If some students find it physically challenging to create diagrams or drawings (e.g., students with physical disabilities), offer a wider range of options. In addition to drawing, students might be given the options of using computer design, sculpting, painting, or creating collages with ripped paper and other materials.
- The spokesperson role should be rotated during the gallery walk so that no one is left without the opportunity to explore and learn from the gallery, or use this role as a way to help a student practice targeted skills. For instance, a middle-school student who needs fluency practice with text could practice a script with a teacher and then be asked to keep his or her role as spokesperson for the entire activity so as to get multiple opportunities to read the description of his poster.

Ideas for Using This Structure in My Classroom 🖊

_____

_____

_____

_____

_____

_____

_____

_____

A IS FOR _____

In this activity, students take a nostalgic trip back to their childhood days. Students will be engaged in a review of the content and creatively represent what they have learned through the familiar structure of the alphabet book.

This structure brings a sense of playfulness into the classroom (especially when used in upper primary grades, middle school, and high school). It also helps students immerse themselves in books, Web sites, and notes as they search through content-based materials to find ideas and words that correspond with each letter of the alphabet.

Directions

- Begin by telling the students that they will be teaching each other class content by creating and sharing alphabet books.
- Students can be given many different materials to use in their creations. Encourage creativity and innovation by allowing different groups to choose different media for their books.
- When they finish creating their books (complete with illustrations, of course), students can read them to one another as a way to further reinforce course content.
- Books can be left in the classroom and used for review and practice at different points during the unit or during the year.

Examples

- Students in a history class were charged with creating alphabet books to represent different areas of study they had covered during the year. One group, assigned the Harlem Renaissance, created a book with the following pages:
  - A is for African American
  - B is for black migration
  - C is for cultural movement
  - D is for drama
  - E is for Edward Burra
  - F is for fiction
- After hearing about this active learning structure, a high school chemistry teacher selected it as the format for a semester exam review project that he entitled, "A Is for Acids, B Is for Bases." His objectives were to help students review conceptual topics taught during the semester by making their own alphabet books. The parameters of the project were to work in partnerships to create a PowerPoint "e-book" of 26 slides that reviewed the topics of thermodynamics, gases, solutions, and acids and bases. Each slide had to contain a title, two or more pictures with explanations, and a three- to four-sentence description of the slide's topic. Grading criteria included elements related to the technical development of a PowerPoint presentation, accuracy of information, and creativity.

- For younger learners in first grade, rather than addressing the whole alphabet, the academic requirements were abbreviated by simply creating books featuring the letters A, B, and C. During a unit about the sea, students were placed in cooperative groups of three members and asked to agree on a sea creature to feature in their book. Each child was assigned one page to write and illustrate. A group that selected dolphins as their topic wrote the following text: "A is for active, because dolphins play and swim fast. B is for beautiful, because they have shiny and smooth skin. C is for cute, because they squeak and have a happy smile." All students in class were given a list of descriptive words starting with an a, b, or c from which to choose. However, each student was required to write, using invented spelling, why they chose that descriptor (e.g., because they have shiny and smooth skin). Alex, a student with significant motor planning and eye-hand coordination difficulty, was a member of the dolphin group. The occupational therapist facilitated the workings of this group while also assisting Alex. Alex was able to dictate his ideas verbally but was unable to write or draw. With the support of the occupational therapist, he typed his dictated response on the computer using an adapted keyboard and selected a graphic image to contribute to the book. The entire group completed their work at the table closest to the classroom computer, so Alex did not need to be separated from this group while completing his portion of the book.

Methods to Maximize Engagement and Participation

- Show students samples of alphabet books. Point out the different styles of art and different formats of the books. This will help some learners brainstorm ideas for their book.
- Brainstorm as a class before constructing the books; have all students shout out possible words and phrases for topics you suggest. You may want to have another student, a paraprofessional, or another teacher write these suggestions down on the board or on chart paper.
- Allow students to have many different options in how they illustrate their work. Some may want to use clip art from the computer, whereas others may choose to create elaborate pen-and-ink drawings. Still others may want to create a photo essay for their book. An art teacher may want to coteach part of this lesson with you so that students can be introduced to the different types of art represented in these texts.
- If some students in the classroom are emerging readers or have individual goals related to literacy, the teacher may want to work with a speech therapist, reading teacher, or other colleague to help the student construct a product that can be used to practice fluency, decoding, and other related skills. This may involve working with the learner and his or her group as they choose the vocabulary for the book and offering strategies to the learner as he or she reads certain passages.

Ideas for Using This Structure in My Classroom ✎

_____

_____

_____

_____

_____

_____

_____

_____

_____

_____

_____

_____

_____

_____

_____

TOP 10 LISTS

Although not every teacher may be as acerbic or quick witted as David Letterman, anyone can bring the energy and fun of this exercise into the classroom to make review, assessment, and end-of-unit or end-of-year reflection more memorable and more meaningful.

Directions

- Put students into groups of about five. Give each group a set of materials, including markers, a piece of chart paper, and possibly old magazines or other scrap paper.
- Ask groups to consider all they learned during a given day, week, lesson, unit, or year. Then tell them to narrow their ideas to 10 and create a formal list of the most important things they learned.
- Give students freedom to create their list in any way they want, but remind them to fill their chart paper and to write using big text because these lists will be shared with the entire class.
- Encourage students to use color and images and to be creative with their language and the text itself (use block letters for important words, underline key concepts). Remind them that these lists will be used to help others learn, remember, and review.
- Ask students to think of a creative way to present their list. They might read it off humorously like a television host or simply display the list and ask classmates to chant the items with them.
- Post the lists around the room for several days (or even weeks) to reinforce reviewed content.

Examples

- A sixth-grade teacher used *Top 10 Lists* to assess student understanding of a unit on fractions. Some of the items on the list included "The least common multiple is the smallest number that two or more numbers will divide into evenly" and "A prime number is a whole number that is only divisible by itself and one." Students spent an entire class period creating the lists and making their posters and another class period presenting their creations to one another. The teacher then posted the lists around the room and around the school, putting one on the classroom ceiling, another on the door, and one in each of the student bathrooms. Although the teacher spent only two weeks on the fractions unit, her students remembered the content long after she taught the unit.
- To extend this activity as a form of celebration, students can generate lists that exemplify positive traits or actions of an individual or group. For example, "The top 10 reasons why Ms. Jones is an awesome teacher," or "The top 10 reasons why Room 506 deserves a pizza party!"

- In another variation, one high school teacher used this structure as a classroom management tool. She began by asking students to generate ideas on what not to do in the classroom. She encouraged students to describe a classroom out of control and encouraged them to be creative and "off the wall." The first entries on the list "Top 10 Ways *Not* to Behave in this Classroom" were

  1. Pretending to be listening to the teacher's lecture while text-messaging your cousin, Jimmy.

  2. Asking to sharpen your pencil 44 times during one class period.

  3. Trying to throw corn chips through another student's hoop earrings.

  4. Riding a pig or other domesticated animal into the classroom.

  After completing this list, students discussed how they would like their classmates to act and how they might convert these ideas into a few simple rules.

Methods to Maximize Engagement and Participation

- Have some students (or all) write their idea down on an index card and bring it to the group in case they forget their ideas when put on the spot.
- Allow artistic or particularly creative students to illustrate or embellish the lists in ways that might help readers of the chart remember the content.
- Preselect a number of pictures that represent key concepts. A student with cognitive disabilities can select one of these pictures that relates to the theme. Next, other group members can write an appropriate caption related to the picture.
- Provide discrete roles for group members that match their strengths by having someone read portions of the text aloud, write specific entries, or check for spelling and grammatical errors before the list is finalized.
- To ensure that everyone contributes something, tell students that each member of the group must generate one idea before the group can work collaboratively to finish the list.

Ideas for Using This Structure in My Classroom 🖋

_____

_____

_____

_____

_____

_____

_____

_____

CATCH!

This high-energy activity borrowed from professional trainer Sharon Bowman (2003) can be used to begin a class if you need to jolt students back into material already covered or at the end of an activity, class, or day if you want to remind students of all they have just learned.

This is a nice closer or celebration strategy for the diverse classroom, as it gives all students an opportunity to talk, it keeps some learners from monopolizing the discussion, and it keeps others from avoiding it. Because the pace and sequence of respondents is controlled by the students, there is an element of surprise that holds the attention of those participating.

Directions

- Ask students to stand in a circle and face one another.
- Announce that you have in your hand a "response object" and that anyone who holds the object will be asked to share something. The device can be anything from a beach ball to a stuffed toy to a rubber eraser. It can be fun to choose something that is related to course content in some way. For instance, in a unit on marine mammals, a teacher had students toss a stuffed whale around the circle. A high school psychology teacher used an inflatable, illustrated brain for the exercise.
- Tell the students that when they catch the object, they need to share something they learned in the day, unit, lesson, or year. Of course, many other prompts or questions would work well with this structure, including
  o Share a question you still have about the content.
  o What is one thing you still want to learn?
  o What was the hardest/most interesting/most forgettable/most exciting/most annoying/most surprising thing you learned?
- When one person has shared a thought, he or she selects another student (one who has not yet shared) in the circle and tosses the object to that person.
- Keep the response object moving around the group until everyone has shared at least one idea.

Implementation Tip ✋

Have students move together in a tight formation so you don't have the object flying across the room, under desks, into furniture or windows, or out of the door. In addition, you might suggest that students make eye contact with a person before throwing it to them or even require that they say the person's name so that individual has time to get ready for the toss.

Examples

- An English teacher used this structure at the end of her classes to have students quickly review the grammar concept she was teaching that day. One day, for instance, she tossed a ball around the classroom and had students name irregular verbs. As students caught the ball they had to either name an irregular verb or repeat one that a classmate named.
- A physical-education middle-school teacher ended all of her units with this structure. It gave her opportunities to review the standards-based content with her students (e.g., rules of games, parts and functions of the body) without breaking from the active and cooperative spirit of her class. When possible, she used objects related to the unit of study, such as a football for the unit on that sport and a plastic puck for the hockey unit.

Methods to Maximize Engagement and Participation

- Tell students to repeat something that they have heard if they cannot think of an idea. Reinforce the idea that student learning is boosted when content is repeated, so learners need not feel embarrassed or frustrated when they can't think of an original idea. Everyone profits when key concepts are heard again (and again).
- Allow students to pass if they need more time to generate an idea.
- Have some students (or all) write their idea down on an index card and bring it into the circle in case they forget their idea when the object comes their way.
- Another format for this game takes the anxiety out of answering a question on the spot and allows for students who are nonverbal to participate. Small groups of students generate ideas in response to a given prompt and record each idea privately on a tape recorder that is equipped with a pressure switch, like the BIGmack (featured in the *Carousel* example). The switch and tape player are positioned in the center of the small-group circle. When a student catches the object, he or she must hit the switch to express one of the ideas generated. There is an element of surprise because no one will know the idea that will be expressed on a given turn.

Ideas for Using This Structure in My Classroom ✐

_____

_____

_____

_____

_____

_____

SIXTY-SECOND COMMERCIAL

This light and entertaining activity borrowed from corporate trainers (Solem & Pike, 1998) works as a memorable review of course material while serving as a fun celebration of a learning experience, a unit, or even a school year. *Sixty-Second Commercial* exploits student knowledge of both television and popular culture and gives dramatic and outgoing students, in particular, opportunities to shine.

Directions

- In small groups, ask students to create a 60-second television commercial that features a class topic. The commercial should, as much as possible, emphasize elements of curriculum, and the ad should contain a slogan to help the group and all others in the class better remember the content (e.g., "Teapot Dome—It's a Scandal, Not a Household Item!").
- Encourage students to act out the commercial using techniques they see on television (e.g., have an expert or celebrity selling the topic, show a happy family, use statistics).
- Give ample time for brainstorming ideas, and provide a box of props that might be used by the groups in their mini-productions.
- Give each team one minute to present its ad to the class.
- After the presentations, ask different students to share what they learned from the ads.

Implementation Tip ✋

Be sure to give students enough time to generate ideas and rehearse. The brainstorming alone may take 20 minutes or more. Although it may be tempting to cut the process short to save time, teachers often find that the activity is one of the things that students remember most about the unit or the class. When students are brainstorming, they are, in essence, thinking about ways to make the information memorable and catchy. In other words, they are doing what good teachers do! Therefore, the time is usually well spent, and although it may be useful to monitor the groups carefully to be sure they are working efficiently, be careful not to cut the creative process too short.

Example

A ninth-grade English teacher had students perform "parts of speech" commercials to prepare them for a final exam. She gave each group a worksheet with information she wanted them to incorporate into their commercials (ensuring that the most critical concepts would be reviewed) and reminded all the groups that the ultimate goal was to create an advertisement that would help fellow students recall the information on the exam. She then reviewed some of the strategies that advertisers use to help people remember their products (e.g., jingles, alliteration, shock, humor). The commercials were successful in that students learned the content while they prepared the ads and then reported that they were easily able to recall slogans from the ads (e.g., "Need to Verb a Noun? Lucky You! Gerund Is in Town!") when they were taking their tests.

Methods to Maximize Engagement and Participation

- Videotape the commercials, and let students who need reinforcement of the content take the tape home as a review.
- To help students who are deaf or hard of hearing, or for those who may need a multimodal approach to instruction, ask groups to use close captioning in their commercials. While the commercial "plays," a student can flip cue cards on the side of the actors, give all learners a copy of the script so everyone can follow along, or share the lines one by one on an overhead projector or computer screen.
- Consider assigning one or two students the role of the director. This person's job is to make sure that the commercials all have different messages and that students will learn something new from each presentation.
- To make sure students are learning the content, you might have groups perform the commercials repeatedly over the course of a week or month. These reruns give everyone (the groups themselves and the audience) several opportunities to learn the content, and it gives the teacher an enjoyable way to punctuate a lesson or wake up a tired group. Another benefit of the repeated commercials is that it gives the teacher a clever way to support learners. Before a test (or even during), the teacher can hum or sing part of a jingle to aid student recall of concepts.

Ideas for Using This Structure in My Classroom ✎

_____

_____

_____

_____

_____

_____

_____

_____

_____

_____

COLLABORATIVE QUIZ

The typical anxiety associated with testing evaporates (or at least is diminished) when students have opportunities not only to construct the test itself but also to work with others to generate the answers. With this low-stress collaborative technique, students can show what they know and even prepare for other, more formal assessments without boredom, tension, or tedium.

Directions

- Take 10 to 15 minutes and ask students to review a chapter from their book or a set of concepts from a unit. Then ask them to develop one or two quiz questions from this material. Inform them that these questions may show up on an assessment that will be given to the whole class.
- Then, informally, ask students to share their questions and provide the related answers (this part of the process serves as a review for the upcoming quiz). At the end of that exercise, collect the questions.
- The following day (or at another time in the future), distribute a quiz that has been assembled entirely from the questions submitted by the students. The familiarity of the material will certainly decrease the usual test-day rumblings, as will the next direction.
- Inform students that they not only created the quiz collaboratively but that they will also take the quiz collaboratively. Break them into pairs or small groups, giving each group one pencil but enough quizzes so that everyone can have their own copy for reading questions and taking notes.
- Ask them to assign a scribe so that only one person is writing, and inform that that only one of the forms can be submitted, so the scribe will be working on the only quiz that the teacher will see.

Implementation Tip ✋

Although it is possible to engage in this structure in one classroom (with students using low voices), it may be easier to manage if groups are able to spread out in separate spaces for the quiz itself. Potential areas for quiz administration include the library, the hallway, the office, and the computer lab.

Example

A fourth-grade teacher used *Collaborative Quiz* to prepare her students for upcoming standardized state tests. Because the mere mention of these tests typically made students feel nervous, lethargic, or both, she used this technique to make test time more social and, therefore, more enjoyable. The teacher was not surprised to learn that the technique also seemed to better prepare students for the test. Having students generate quiz questions seemed to grab their interest. Giving them time to talk, both about content and the testing situation itself, appeared to promote deeper learning. She was especially impressed with the comments she heard from students as they discussed the final question on the test (the one question she had generated herself): "Share one strategy you use to succeed on tests." In sharing this information, learners were not only able to prepare for the content they would see on the future test, they were also able to share concrete learning strategies. This sharing helped them all, and in particular helped students who didn't traditionally do well in testing situations.

Methods to Maximize Engagement and Participation

- To generate more interest for students, allow them to submit test questions written as answers (in the style of the television game show *Jeopardy!*). Some students will be motivated by the novelty of such a task and may even come up with more complex material due to the unique challenge.

- Before generating questions on their own, some students will need to see sample questions related to the material being studied and examples of different types of quiz questions (e.g., matching, true/false, multiple-choice, and fill in the blank). For students who need even more support to generate ideas, a sample quiz with several questions could be provided, and these learners could be asked to highlight the one or two questions they would like to see on the quiz. The sample questions can be coded as easy, medium, or high difficulty levels.

- On quiz day, be sure that the student assigned to be the scribe will be able to handle the task of writing on demand and organizing thoughts and ideas quickly. If this task will be challenging for many of the students in the group, consider assigning the role to multiple students with each taking a short turn. You might also assign other roles, such as time keeper, proofreader, collaboration monitor, and encourager.

Ideas for Using This Structure in My Classroom ✐

_____

_____

_____

_____

_____

_____

_____

_____

_____

_____

_____

HUMAN TREASURE HUNT

Many camp counselors, scout leaders, and church group organizers have used this activity to break the ice at a meeting or to inspire laughter at a social gathering. *Human Treasure Hunt* can include simple to complex questions and can include both personal questions (e.g., find someone who wears socks to bed) and questions related to classroom content (e.g., find someone who knows who the two U.S. senators from Wyoming are). This structure lends itself to assessing and celebrating because it affirms the expertise of the members of the classroom before or after learning new material has taken place.

Directions

- In this simple game, students are given a worksheet with a series of questions or prompts related to course content. The objective is for students to find an answer to every prompt on their treasure hunt form by soliciting information from other class members.
- Distribute the worksheets and announce the simple rules for the game: (a) you can get only one answer from each student you approach, and (b) if you get an answer from another student, you need to give an answer to him or her.
- Students are then directed to take these sheets and walk around the room, interacting with multiple members of the class and securing answers to the questions.

Implementation Tip ✋

To get students moving immediately, tell them they are not allowed to work with anyone in their row (or table) for the first two or three items of the treasure hunt. You may even want to be more specific; if you want to get students out of their desks and away from the partners they traditionally choose, you can assign partners for the first few items of the hunt.

Example

A high school science teacher asked students to complete a human treasure hunt as an end-of-quarter review (see Figure 5.2). All students were asked to contribute potential questions for the hunt, and the teacher constructed the worksheet entirely from student-generated items. As students circulated around the room, gathering information from one another, the teacher listened in on conversations to assess readiness for the exam and to provide individual students with on-the-spot instruction on key points. Randy, a young man with exceptional ability in science, already knew most of the concepts on the sheet before beginning the exercise, so the teacher allowed him to replace three questions with three new "challenge prompts" that he pulled from outside reading and from a quick search on the classroom computer. Randy was then allowed to approach individual students with these enrichment questions as part of the treasure hunt activity.

Figure 5.2 Human Treasure Hunt: Physical Science Example

Human Treasure Hunt

The goal of this activity is to learn as much as you can from the experts in this classroom. You may get only one answer from each person you approach, and that person may get only one answer from you.

1. Find a person who can draw a picture of "a force acting through a distance" (work).

Have this artist sign here: _____

2. Find someone who can name a use of radioactivity.

_____

Have this science expert sign here: _____

3. Find someone who can explain a type of pulley you use in everyday life.

_____

_____

Have this observant classmate sign here: _____

4. Find someone who will act out, explain, or draw the Doppler effect.

Have this creative individual sign here: _____

After you are finished, walk around the room and help your classmates finish their treasure hunts.

Methods to Maximize Engagement and Participation

- Have a few students serve as "hunt helpers." Their job is to walk around and offer assistance to students who are having difficulty completing their forms. Helpers can provide information or, preferably, point students to others who have expertise in certain areas and who may have helped other students with the same item on the hunt form.
- Let students generate a few of their own items as they wander around the room or before the hunt begins.
- If a peer cannot answer a question verbally, his or her classmate can invent a question that can be answered by gesturing, drawing, or pointing to items in the classroom or in the textbook. A question such as "Find someone who can sign the elements that make up water (H_2O)" pushes every student to learn alternative ways of expressing their knowledge.
- Students who have specific skills, who have mastered selected content, or who have a limited repertoire of facts can rehearse unique information on which they are experts in advance of this activity. Prompts can be written on other students' treasure hunt forms to alert them to their classmate's expertise. For example, "Remember to ask Jim about the symbol for iron and helium," or "Dagne and Russ both know about Sacagawea's role on the Lewis and Clark expedition."
- Some students may be given fewer items to find on their scavenger hunt list if communication or movement issues affect their speed in acquiring information, or students may be given different questions (all hunt forms do not need to be the same); some students may be asked to find answers to less-complex questions than others.
- Allow students needing more challenge to create the hunt form for the group.
- Allow students to peek at their textbook or class notes if they need assistance to answer a question.
- This activity gives teachers an opportunity to highlight the expertise, specific gifts, or strengths of individual learners. If a student has just moved from Saudi Arabia, the teacher might include an item related to the geography of the Middle East. If a book-loving student has a particular interest in *Alice in Wonderland*, the treasure hunt might include an item asking students to act out or draw a scene from the popular book.

Ideas for Using This Structure in My Classroom 🖊

_____

_____

_____

_____

_____

_____

ACT LIKE IT!

This classroom game, although silly, often helps learners retain information they otherwise might not. In this activity, students work in small teams to "become" words, concepts, ideas, or things. Teachers can either assign all groups the same word or concept or give different groups different (but related) words or concepts. Depending on the students' needs, the teacher may choose to offer options that are very concrete, such as "pyramid" or "microscope," or ones that are more abstract and complex, such as "community," "element," "cosine," or "imagery."

Directions

- Ask students to represent a word, concept, or an idea that is relevant to the curriculum and can help them demonstrate their knowledge. You can set aside a portion of the class period and assign different concepts to each group of students or ask every group to illustrate the same concept.
- The assigned referents might be known to everyone in the room, or each group might have a secret identity that must be guessed by observing groups. The prompt is given to each group, either verbally or in writing. For instance, a group might get this assignment: "You are the desert ecosystem. Act like it!"
- Give groups a short period of time to generate ideas for a performance; this version sometimes can be fun, as students need to think on their feet and react based on the most salient points in their mind.
- Another way to engineer the activity is to give learners time to plan and treat the performances more like a formal review. In this version, you can give specific criteria. For instance, you might require that the performances last at least a minute and that students use at least two props as they perform.

Examples

- In a ninth-grade science lesson, a teacher asked his students, in groups of four, to act out the concept of "fusion" and "fission." Although all of the learners essentially engaged in the same types of behaviors when they performed (rushing together into a clump and then fleeing to all corners of the classroom), each group had its own interpretation, and each mini-presentation helped the students remember the movement of atoms in each of the examples come exam time.
- In a language arts lesson, the teacher asked students to act like the following vocabulary words: *evocative, nefarious, pithy, onerous, precocious, sordid,* and *restitution.* Each group had to act out each one of the words while the audience guessed which skit represented which word from the list. This exercise was especially useful for Renee, a student with Asperger's syndrome. Renee found the visual imagery helpful to learn new words (especially those with abstract meanings). The lighthearted atmosphere of the activity helped her feel relaxed, which was a contrast

to the feeling of stress she experienced in other language-laden academic experiences.

Methods to Maximize Engagement and Participation

- Provide a box of costumes and props for students to use in their acts, or give students items such as scrap paper, blankets, paper towels, ribbons, paper plates, and school supplies and ask them to create props on the spot.
- For students who need more challenge, assign charades that are more abstract or allow these learners to write their own *Act Like It!* prompts.
- To further student learning, ask students to engage in impromptu revisions of each scene. You could put students into groups that have various jobs related to improving the short skits. For instance, one group might be asked to fact check and another might suggest helpful visuals. Still another might work on sound (e.g., suggest dialogue or certain types of music) to extend the meaning of the scene.

Ideas for Using This Structure in My Classroom ✏

References

Bennett, B., Rolheiser, C., & Stevahn, L. (1991). *Cooperative learning: Where heart meets mind.* Toronto, Canada: Educational Connections.

Bonwell, C., & Eisen, J. (1991, September). *Active learning: Creating excitement in the classroom* (ED340272). Washington, DC: George Washington University.

Bowman, S. (2003). *How to give it so they get it.* Glenbrook, NV: Bowperson.

Boyle, J. (2001). Enhancing the note-taking skills of students with mild disabilities. *Intervention in School and Clinic, 36,* 221–224.

Cole, R. (2001). *More strategies for educating everybody's children.* Alexandria, VA: Association for Supervision and Curriculum Development.

Core-Plus Mathematics Project. (2005). *CPMP Course 1 units.* Retrieved June 20, 2007, from http://www.wmich.edu/cpmp/

Davidson, E., & Schniedewind, N. (1998). *Open minds to equality: A sourcebook of learning activities to affirm diversity and promote equity* (2nd ed.). Needham Heights, MA: Allyn & Bacon.

Draper, R. (1997). Active learning in mathematics: Desktop teaching. *Mathematics Teacher, 90,* 622–625.

Falvey, M., Givner, C., & Kimm, C. (1995). What is an inclusive school? In R. Villa & J. Thousand (Eds.), *Creating an inclusive school* (pp. 1–12). Alexandria, VA: Association for Supervision and Curriculum Development.

Fisher, D., & Roach, V. (1999). *Opening doors: Connecting students to curriculum, classmates, and learning.* Colorado Springs, CO: PEAK Parent Center.

Fisher, D., Sax, C., & Pumpian, I. (1999). *Inclusive high schools: Learning from contemporary classrooms.* Baltimore: Paul H. Brookes.

Freire, P. (1970). *Pedagogy of the oppressed.* New York: Continuum.

Gadotti, M. (1994). *Reading Paulo Freire: His life & work.* Albany, NY: State University of New York Press.

Gibbs, J. (1995). *Tribes: A new way of learning and being together.* Sausalito, CA: Center Source Systems.

Harmin, M. (1994). *Inspiring active learning: A handbook for teachers.* Alexandria, VA: Association for Supervision and Curriculum Development.

Harmin, M., & Toth, M. (2006). *Inspiring active learning: A complete handbook for today's teacher.* Alexandria, VA: Association for Supervision and Curriculum Development.

Harry, B., & Klinger, J. (2005). *Why are so many minority students in special education? Understanding race & disability in schools.* New York: Teachers College Press.

Howard, P. (1994). *Owner's manual for the brain.* Austin, TX: Leorinian Press.

Jensen, E. (1998). *Teaching with the brain in mind.* Alexandria, VA: Association for Supervision and Curriculum Development.

Johnson, D. W., Johnson, R. T., & Smith, K. A. (1998). *Active learning: Cooperation in the college classroom* (2nd ed.). Edina, MN: Interaction Book.

Jorgensen, C. (1998). *Restructuring high schools for all students: Taking inclusion to the next level.* Baltimore: Paul H. Brookes.

Kagan, S. (1992). *Cooperative learning.* San Clemente, CA: Kagan.

Kasa-Hendrickson, C., & Kluth, P. (2005). "We have to start with inclusion and work it out as we go": Purposeful inclusion for non-verbal students with autism. *International Journal of Whole Schooling, 2*(1), 2–14.

Kluth, P. (2003). *"You're going to love this kid": Teaching students with autism in the inclusive classroom.* Baltimore: Paul H. Brookes.

Kluth, P., Straut, D., & Biklen, D. (Eds.). (2003). *Access to academics for all students: Critical approaches to inclusive curriculum, instruction, and policy.* Mahweh, NJ: Erlbaum.

Loomans, D., & Kolberg, K. (1993). *The laughing classroom: Everyone's guide to teaching with humor and play.* Tiburon, CA: H. J. Kramer.

Margulies, N., & Maal, N. (2001). *Mapping inner space: Learning and teaching visual mapping.* Chicago: Zephyr Press.

Marzano, R. (2003).*What works in schools: Translating research into action.* Alexandria, VA: Association for Supervision and Curriculum Development.

Oyler, C. (2001). Democratic classrooms and accessible instruction. *Democracy & Education, 14,* 28–31.

Panitz, T. (1997). Collaborative versus cooperative learning: Comparing the two definitions helps understand the nature of interactive learning. *Cooperative Learning and College Teaching, 8*(2).

Parker, J. (1990). *Workshops for active learning.* Vancouver, Canada: JFP Productions.

Rossi, E. L., & Nimmons, D. (1991). *The 20-minute break: Using the new science of ultradian rhythms.* Los Angeles: Tarcher.

Ruhl, K., Hughes, C., & Schloss, P. (1987). Using the pause procedure to enhance lecture recall. *Teacher Education and Special Education, 10,* 14–18.

Russell, I. J., Hendricson, W. D., & Herbert, R. J. (1984). Effects of lecture information density on medical student achievement. *Journal of Medical Education, 59,* 881–889.

Sapon-Shevin, M. (1999). *Because we can change the world: A practical guide to building cooperative, inclusive classroom communities.* Boston: Allyn & Bacon.

Sapon-Shevin, M. (2007). *Widening the circle: The power of inclusive classrooms.* Boston, MA: Beacon Press.

Short, K. G., Harste, J., & Burke, C. (1996). *Creating classrooms for authors and inquirers* (2nd ed.). Portsmouth, NH: Heinemann.

Silberman, M. (1996). *Active learning: 101 strategies to teach any subject.* Boston: Allyn & Bacon.

Solem, L., & Pike, B. (1998). *50 creative training closers: Innovative ways to end your training with IMPACT.* San Francisco: Jossey-Bass.

Tomlinson, C. (1995). *How to differentiate instruction in mixed-ability classrooms.* Alexandria, VA: ASCD.

Tomlinson, C. (2003). *Fulfilling the promise of the differentiated classroom: Strategies and tools for responsive teaching.* Alexandria, VA: Association for Supervision and Curriculum Development.

Udvari-Solner, A. (1993). *Curricular adaptations: Accommodating the instructional needs of diverse learners in the context of general education classrooms* (Rev. ed.). Topeka: Kansas State Department of Education.

Udvari-Solner, A. (1995). A process for adapting curriculum in inclusive classrooms. In R. Villa & J. Thousand (Eds.), *Creating an inclusive school* (pp. 110–124). Alexandria, VA: Association for Supervision and Curriculum Development.

Udvari-Solner, A. (1996a). Examining teacher thinking: Constructing a process to design curricular adaptations. *Remedial and Special Education, 17,* 245–254.

Udvari-Solner, A. (1996b). Theoretical influences on the establishment of inclusive practices. *Cambridge Journal of Education, 26*(1), 101–119.

Udvari-Solner, A. (1997). Inclusive education. In C. Grant & G. Ladson-Billings (Eds.), *The dictionary of multi-cultural education* (pp. 141–144). Phoenix, AZ: Oryx Press.

Udvari-Solner, A. (2003). Leading social change in collaborative and inclusive practice: The journey of a middle school. *Impact: Feature Issue on Revisiting Inclusive K–12 Education, 16*(1). Retrieved June 20, 2007, from http://ici.umn.edu/products/impact/161/prof3.html

Udvari-Solner, A., & Thousand, J. (1996). Creating a responsive curriculum for inclusive schools. *Remedial and Special Education, 17,* 182–192.

Udvari-Solner, A., Villa, R., & Thousand, J. (2002). Access to the general education curriculum for all: The universal design process. In J. Thousand, R. Villa, & A. Nevin (Eds), *Creativity and collaboration: A practical guide to empowering students and teachers* (pp. 85–103). Baltimore: Paul H. Brookes.

Udvari-Solner, A., Villa, R., & Thousand, J. (2005). Access to the general education curriculum for all: The universal design process. In R. Villa & J. Thousand (Eds.), *Creating an inclusive school* (2nd ed., pp. 134–155). Alexandria, VA: Association for Supervision and Curriculum Development.

Villa, R., & Thousand, J. (Eds.). (2005). *Creating an inclusive school* (2nd ed.) Alexandria, VA: Association for Supervision and Curriculum Development.

Vygotsky, L. S. (1978). *Mind in society.* Cambridge, MA: Harvard University Press.

Index

CORWIN PRESS

The Corwin Press logo—a raven striding across an open book—represents the union of courage and learning. Corwin Press is committed to improving education for all learners by publishing books and other professional development resources for those serving the field of PreK–12 education. By providing practical, hands-on materials, Corwin Press continues to carry out the promise of its motto: **"Helping Educators Do Their Work Better."**